DELAWARE
Patriot Heroes

DELAWARE
Patriot Heroes

ROBERT KIRKWOOD AND PETER JAQUETT

BRIGADIER GENERAL KENNARD R. WIGGINS JR.
(DE ANG, RET.)

THE
History
PRESS

Published by The History Press
Charleston, SC
www.historypress.com

Cover images: Eighteenth-century Hessian map of the Philadelphia Campaign. *Operations of the royal army in North America under the orders of Sir William Howe, Knight of the Order of Bath. From the descent at Elk Ferry 25 August until taking possession of Philadelphia 26 September, 1777 against the American Rebels commanded by Mr. Washington and other commanders.* Designed by Ensign Cochenhausen. *Wikimedia Commons*; *Battle of Long Island*, depicting the Delaware Regiment at the Battle of Long Island on August 27, 1776. A National Guard Heritage Painting by twenty-first-century artist Domenick D'Andrea, created for the National Guard Bureau. *Wikimedia Commons.*

First published 2024

Manufactured in the United States

ISBN 9781467156868

Library of Congress Control Number: 2023950477

Notice: The information in this book is true and complete to the best of our knowledge. It is offered without guarantee on the part of the author or The History Press. The author and The History Press disclaim all liability in connection with the use of this book.

This book is dedicated to the sons and daughters of the American Revolution who maintain the memory and heritage of our Patriot heroes for future generations.

CONTENTS

FOREWORD

I am greatly honored to have been asked to write the foreword to this new and valuable addition to the body of scholarship about Delaware's Revolutionary War history that highlights two underappreciated participants: Captain Peter Jaquett and Captain Robert Kirkwood.

In *Delaware Patriot Heroes: Robert Kirkwood and Peter Jaquett*, General Wiggins has painstakingly drawn on both known and hitherto largely unknown information about these two "battle buddies" in the Revolutionary War—how apt a term.

It made perfect sense for General Wiggins to have combined the life stories of Peter Jaquett and Robert Kirkwood into one book. As Wiggins notes, "They were good friends and comrades" during the war. Notably, the wartime experiences of each man give important context to understanding the life and times of the other man.

It is very fitting that two chapters of the Delaware Sons of the American Revolution are named for Peter Jaquett and Robert Kirkwood, and it is equally fitting that the Delaware SAR has been so supportive of this important project. The lives of Peter Jaquett and Robert Kirkwood needed to be told in full. And Wiggins has done this well.

This very readable book brings alive the Revolutionary War sacrifices and valor of not just Peter Jaquett and Robert Kirkwood but of all patriots and citizens of Delaware and of the fledgling United States of America who, against great odds, secured "liberty and independence" for the emerging new nation.

Lastly, I cannot refrain from mentioning that this small task of authoring this foreword has been particularly pleasurable for me since Peter Jaquett and I share a common ancestor, Jean Paul Jaquett, vice director and chief magistrate of the Dutch settlement at New Castle.

To General Wiggins and the Delaware SAR: well done!

RICHARD RODNEY COOCH
Delaware Superior Court Judge (Ret.)
New Castle, Delaware
October 2023

ACKNOWLEDGEMENTS

The author would like to thank the Peter Jaquett Chapter of the Sons of the American Revolution for the initial inspiration to write this book. Its interest and support have been invaluable to this effort. I would especially like to thank Robert Reed, who was my initial contact. His engaging and friendly manner was a great cover for an iron will to see that the history of the chapter's namesake would be rediscovered and retaught to future generations. Robert got the ball rolling, and before I realized it, I had been pulled into a new and rewarding quest that shared his enthusiasm.

A team was created to discuss the form this effort would take, and it has turned out to be a panel of excellence, drawing from a deep talent pool. I want to especially thank Harry Thomes, Noel Kuhrt, John Ebenreiter, Kim Burdick and Paul Bechly, all of whom served as the strategic planners, executive editors, financial advisors, eagle-eyed proofreaders and producers of this enterprise. They have taken what had been a few paragraphs in the SAR history and made it into a suitable and lasting monument for two great American patriots. Their labors and the resources of the Peter Jaquett Chapter have made this book possible.

I'd also like to thank the Delaware Military Museum Library and Archives. It provided invaluable resources, records and publications that were the foundation of this project's scholarship. I am grateful to Richard Cooch for his enthusiastic contribution to Delaware history.

Finally, my special gratitude to my darling wife, Elizabeth, who not only patiently endures my enthusiasms but also actually helps to enable them.

INTRODUCTION

I was asked to give a talk on Peter Jaquett by the Peter Jaquett Chapter of the Sons of the American Revolution a few years ago. The beginnings of this project originated with that request. I knew little about Jaquett. I reviewed the available published literature on Delaware's role in the Revolution, supplemented by some web surfing, and produced a little essay that became the basis of my talk. Later, I was asked to give a second talk to a joint gathering that included the Robert Kirkwood Chapter of the SAR. So, my talk expanded to include new material about Captain Kirkwood, again based on an expanded paper. I have included citations for my sources in the endnotes.[1]

This project was meant to be a lark, a minor diversion. Yet I became fascinated by these Delaware Patriots and their story. As a writer, one keeps finding that one last little nugget of truth as one sifts through the research. I began to feel a personal affinity for these fellows and, despite the span of centuries, got to know them a little. So this work is, and always will be, a "work in progress" as I come across new information.

In modern terms, Captains Kirkwood and Jaquett were "battle buddies." They were good friends and comrades. They assisted each other on and off the field of battle. They were partners in the great enterprise of a war to win our nation's independence. They had a shared experience—and a difficult and challenging experience it had been. No bond is stronger than one formed in adversity and hardship. They both shared these travails in abundance. The result was that both men shared a common commitment to duty, honor and country.

In writing biography, one researches as much as one is able in order to build a chronology of the events of a life. When the subject is from the eighteenth century, the historical record can be frustratingly patchy and brief. Although there are volumes of papers and correspondence on my subjects, much of it consists of lists of soldiers, accounts of expenses and tallies of supplies expended. There is a lot of raw material, but it often fails to illuminate the soul of the man.

Captain Jaquett appears to be a man of few recorded words. Much of what we have in the historiography is secondhand, recorded by others about him, but not much from the captain himself. In retirement, Jaquett wrote about his war experience, but years after the fact. These writings came in the form of appeals for pensions and for government positions, relating his activities for the record.

Captain Kirkwood, on the other hand, was a fine and prolific writer. He kept a daily journal and order book that recorded many details of the distances marched, highlights of activities and his correspondence from the field on military matters. A surviving letter to his father reveals his gift for storytelling.

Nevertheless, one forms impressions after intently studying a subject. You get to know them in a certain sense. I began to contrast and compare the two soldiers. Without hard evidence, here are the qualities I began to form in my mind's eye.

Peter Jaquett was the solid rock. He was the man you want in your foxhole with you for steadfast support. He was an unflappable soldier. He was not especially well educated and articulate, but he was utterly reliable and calm under pressure. Jaquett was loyal and firm in his beliefs. He may have been quarrelsome and boastful, but he could endure hardship and defeat with equanimity. He was the perfect counterpoint to Kirkwood. They reinforced each other's strengths. In death, Jaquett was mourned as a genuine hero by his community, but he was largely forgotten by history. I hope you will find him as interesting as I did.

The Peter Jaquett I discovered was a gentleman farmer, down a little at the heels, turned soldier of necessity. He served bravely and loyally and was an evident natural leader. He suffered great defeats and hardships but also tasted the nectar of victory. Jaquett returned to his family home a man broken physically and found a ruined farm with debts and obligations. Nevertheless, he was an active participant in his community, and his leadership skills remained with him as a pillar of the community. Perhaps suffering from what we today might term post-traumatic stress disorder (PTSD), he was described as a "cross, morose, quarrelsome man. It was hard for anyone to keep on speaking terms."[2] He was a man of contradictions who wrongly sued a neighbor yet loved children. He was a natural leader but seemed to have difficulty in gaining a government appointment. Jaquett was a raconteur of his tales as a soldier and held his audience spellbound with his many stories.

Kirkwood was charismatic. It seems almost every reference to him in the historical record dubs him the "Gallant Kirkwood." His troops called him "Captain Bob." He was respected and known to be a disciplinarian, both for those he commanded as well as for himself. He led from the front and he led by example. He was bold and resourceful. He was a man who could think on his feet and anticipate the next move of the enemy. Kirkwood was a skilled tactician. No physical description of him survives, but I'd bet he was athletic and agile in his person. He was called a "man of steel" and was to march thousands of miles. Kirkwood was a natural leader who had attractive qualities. He must have had extraordinary people skills to recruit soldiers and convince them of his cause. You would want to follow his lead and trust him with your life. Kirkwood has been called "America's first combat infantryman," serving as the model for what an American soldier ought to be.[3]

Captain Kirkwood appears to have been prone to disease, and there are several mentions of the "ague" that laid him low. Despite his maladies, he took risks and was willing to seize the initiative. In the end, this physical vulnerability was to be partially responsible for his fall.

These two Patriots are remarkable for their courageous military deeds and their loyal longevity. By itself this record of accomplishment across thirty-two battles, spanning almost eight years, would be noteworthy. But when placed in the context of hardship, poverty, starvation, disease, deprivation and exhausting physical exertion, as you will see in these pages, it is nothing less than extraordinary.

Chapter 1

JAQUETT AND KIRKWOOD
FAMILY HISTORIES

Jean Paul Jaquet (circa 1620–circa 1684)

The first, and apparently only, Jaquet (pronounced *zhe-ket* in the original French) to immigrate to America was Jean Paul Jaquet. He was a Protestant whose French family had fled to avoid religious persecution. Jean Paul Jaquet was born in Nuremberg, Bavaria, about 1615–20. He moved to Holland and became connected with the Dutch West India Company, with service in Brazil. We write about his immigration to "America" because Jean Paul Jaquet first lived in what is now the eastern tip of Brazil, South America, from 1646 or a bit earlier until January 1654, before briefly returning to Amsterdam. He arrived in the American Dutch colonies on the ship *de Grote Christoffel* before April 1655. Jean Paul married Maria de Carpentier, of a reasonably well-connected Amsterdam family, in Brazil in 1646. They had a son, Peter, in 1649. Therein lies the connection to the Dutch West India Company in Brazil: Jean Paul Jaquet became (the last) governor of the company's holdings in Brazil sometime after 1644.

Peter Stuyvesant was governor-general, spending most of his time in New Amsterdam (New York City today), and needed a strong number-two man to supervise in his absence. Jaquet became the first vice-director of Delaware under the Dutch rule in 1655. Once in New Amsterdam, Governor Petrus (Peter) Stuyvesant of New Amsterdam granted Jean Paul Jaquet land and subsequently made him a vice-director, responsible for the holdings on the

South River, now the (lower) Delaware River. It seems to have been the same land (two hundred acres) granted to him by William Penn in 1682 after title to the area passed to Penn.

Jaquet took residence at Fort Casimir in New Castle, Delaware. He was to command all officers, soldiers and freemen in the colony. The vice-director was to keep Fort Casimir in a state of defense, to see that the fort was properly guarded and to supervise the training and discipline of the soldiers.[4] His modern-day equivalent is the adjutant general for Delaware, the leader of the Delaware National Guard. Fort Casimir became the new seat of the colony. This land was granted to Jaquet soon after the capture of Delaware by the Dutch.

Thus, Jean Paul Jaquet was present for both the capitulation of the Dutch West India Company in Brazil to the Portuguese (1654) and of the Dutch American colonies (lower Delaware River) to the British (1664).[5]

Jean Paul Jaquet was alive in February 1684, but he was listed as deceased by July 1685.

Jaquett Line of Descendency

Jean Paul Jaquet, 1620–1685, m. Marie de Carpentier
Peter Jaquett I, 1649–1726, m. Ingeborg Stedham
Peter Jaquett II, 1688–1744, m. Marta Jaquett
Peter Jaquett Sr., 1718–1772, m. Elizabeth Price
Major Peter Jaquett, 1755–1834, m. Elizabeth Jaquett

LONG HOOK

Jean Paul Jaquet was given a farm of 290 acres called Long Hook with an original survey dating to 1681. It was described as "across from the Rocks along the southern side of the Christina River where it forms a point, south of Wilmington." It stood on a rise overlooking the Christina Marsh (once called Holland Marsh). It was conveniently located between south Wilmington and New Castle. He built a frame house there with a brick fireplace where Routes 13 and I-495 meet today, at 1051 South Market Street.[6]

Long Hook farmhouse circa 1930, east elevation, Long Hook Farm, 1051 South Market Street, Wilmington, New Castle County, Delaware. *Library of Congress (HABS DEL,2-WILM.V,2—1).*

Long Hook Farm, south elevation. *Library of Congress (HABS DEL,2-WILM.V,2—2).*

A descendant, James Day Howson Jr., described the house in this way:

Long Hook Farm was partly brick and partly framed, painted yellow. On the grounds are a pair of ancient mahogany trees. The oldest part of the house, a frame wing of wide vertical planks covering the structural timbers, contains a great fireplace and floorboards twenty-two inches wide. It is believed to have been built about 1660. Peter Jaquett (father of Major Jaquett) added the brick wing in 1763. The last additions made about 1800, included an extension of the main wing and an additional story on both wings. The walls still show clearly the heights and lines of the original gables.[7]

In 1699, Dankers and Sluyter Labadist crossed the Christina near to this farm. They spoke of it as follows:

We proceeded thence a small distance overland to a place where the fortress of Christina had stood, which had been constructed and possessed by the Swedes, but taken by the Dutch governor, Stuyvesant, and afterwards, I believe, demolished by the English. We were then taken over the Christina Creek in a canoe, and landed at the spot where Stuyvesant threw up his battery to attack the fort, and compelled them to surrender. At this spot there are medlar trees, which bear good fruit, from which one Jaquett, who does not live far from there, makes good brandy or spirits, which we tasted and found even better than French brandy.[8]

Major Peter Jaquett

Major Peter Jaquett was born at Long Hook Farm on April 6, 1755, son of Peter Jaquett and Elizabeth. At maturity, he was described as a "small, thick-set man."

Like his father (the great-grandson of Jean Paul), young Peter tilled the land. Farming was very hard work. The men toiled all day in the fields. Long Hook was known for its rich bottomland soil and cattle. Some of the crops were rice, indigo, flax, grains and lots of fruits and vegetables. Peter had access to books and attended school. The farm offered Peter the opportunity to learn nature, sportsmanship, angling, boat handling and an appreciation for music. When he turned seven, his father reminded him that

Long Hook (Kent Manor Inn), circa 1950, east front, Long Hook Farm. *Library of Congress (HABS DEL, 2-WILM. V, 2—3).*

"the Buttonwood trees will grow as you grow, shade you in declining years, and long survive, and annually renew their verdure."[9]

In 1763, the elder Peter Jaquett added an addition to the house. On it he engraved his initials and the date in brick headers on the south end of the structure. The home was at all times a social center. It was known far and wide, and many enjoyed its hospitality. Its guests later included Washington, Lafayette and Bishop White. The house was enlarged once again just prior to the Civil War.[10]

A beautiful ivy vine covered one end of the house. It was gathered from the castle where Mary Queen of Scots was imprisoned and presented to Major Jaquett's wife.[11] The property included lofty poplars, evergreens and an immense weeping willow with a hanging bird's nest. The first "Campney" roses planted by Mrs. Jaquett entered the eaves to the attic and bloomed throughout the winter.

The original property of 290 acres was eventually subdivided and sold off over the decades. The manor home and its grounds fell into disrepair,

Peter Jaquett.
Delaware Society
of the Sons of
the American
Revolution.

especially in the years between the Great War and the Great Depression. By 1930, there remained only 16 acres and a house in very poor condition.

In 1940, restaurateur James Boines bought the property and upgraded the interior. The original building ended its days as a restaurant and lounge with an adjacent motel. In its heyday, it was described as an overflow for the posher Hotel DuPont uptown. It was the site of a campaign luncheon by John F. Kennedy on October 8, 1958.[12] Boines retired in 1976 and leased the inn until 1982. It was closed in 1983 and operated as a nightclub for teenagers for a short time. In October 5, 1986, a fire broke out in the vacant building.[13] The burnt ruins were later razed.

MAJOR ROBERT KIRKWOOD

The elder Robert Kirkwood was of Scottish descent and was born near Derry in Ireland. In 1731, at about age eighteen to twenty, the elder Robert Kirkwood immigrated to North America in the company of the widow and two infant children of his deceased brother, William. Some years after his arrival, Robert married Sara McDowell, a native of England who was a member of the religious Society of Friends. They lived on a farm about two miles north of Newark adjacent to where the White Clay Creek Presbyterian Church now stands at the corner of the aptly named Kirkwood Highway and Polly Drummond Road. They had nine children, all daughters excepting only Robert Kirkwood the younger, born in 1756.[14]

Although the elder Kirkwood's occupation was "yeoman farmer," it's clear that he was a substantial member of his community, as well as a thoroughgoing Patriot. Kirkwood farmed a homestead in New Castle County and served as an elder in White Clay Creek Presbyterian Church.

White Clay Creek Presbyterian Church, Robert Kirkwood Highway and Polly Drummond Hill Road, Newark, New Castle County, Delaware. *Library of Congress (HABS DEL,2-NEWARK.V,1—1).*

In May 1775, Kirkwood Sr. was part of a committee of correspondence composed of justices of the peace and grand jurors who were tasked with raising money for "our suffering brethren at Boston."[15]

Not much is known about Major Kirkwood's childhood. Family tradition holds that he was a precocious scholar; if his reputation and diary entries are any indication, he was raised with a rigid sense of duty and rectitude. Robert Kirkwood studied classical studies and religion with great diligence and success at the Newark Academy, intending to become a minister.

In January 1776, the Delaware Council of Safety complied with Congress's request to raise a single regiment for service in the Continental army. Among the well-connected young men who received commissions in the regiment was Robert Kirkwood, who was appointed a first lieutenant on January 17.[16] He was placed under the command of Colonel John Haslet.

Chapter 2

THE DELAWARE CONTINENTALS

*O*n December 9, 1775, the Continental Congress called on the Lower Counties in Delaware to furnish a battalion (at that time, an interchangeable term for a regiment) of infantry for one year's service in the Continental army. Recruiting began in January, and by April 12, 1776, muster rolls recorded six companies in Dover and two companies in Lewistown (Lewes).

Colonel John Haslet's Delaware Regiment of Foot in the service of the United States of America, also known simply as the Delaware Regiment or Delaware Battalion, was the original organization formed in January 1776—eight companies of about 750 men. Haslet was a tall, wiry, athletic Ulsterman, educated in Glasgow and ordained as a Presbyterian minister before immigrating to America, where he fought the French. He became a physician in Delaware.[17] The men enlisted for a term of one year, expiring on January 1, 1777.

Answering the call to arms by the Delaware Counsel for Public Safety, at age twenty, Peter Jaquett served from January 1776 to the end of the war, spending but six weeks at home in all that time. He was in thirty-two battles and many skirmishes and was twice wounded, although not severely. He served throughout, alongside his friend and comrade Robert Kirkwood. In every general engagement that was fought between New York and Charleston, Kirkwood commanded the First Company and Jaquett the Second Company of the Delaware Regiment, fighting shoulder to shoulder.

Colonel John Haslet's Delaware Regiment, depicting a private, a captain and another private. *Delaware Military Museum.*

Here is the oath that Kirkwood and Jaquett would have taken, as written by the Continental Congress in October 1776:

I _____, do acknowledge the Thirteen United States of America, namely, New Hampshire, Massachusetts Bay, Rhode Island, Connecticut, New York, New Jersey, Pennsylvania, Delaware, Maryland, Virginia, North

Carolina, South Carolina, and Georgia, to be free, independent, and sovereign states, and declare, that the people thereof owe no allegiance or obedience to George the third, king of Great Britain; and I renounce, refuse and abjure any allegiance or obedience to him; and I do swear that I will, to the utmost of my power, support, maintain, and defend the said United States against the said king, George the third, and his heirs and successors, and his and their abettors, assistants and adherents; and will serve the said United States in the office of _____, which I now hold, and in any other office which I may hereafter hold by their appointment, or under their authority, with fidelity and honour, and according to the best of my skill and understanding. So help me God.

An essay that appeared in Kirkwood's journal that summer revealed his thoughts as he set out for service that could very well cost him his life. He regarded the Revolution as an epic contest for liberty and expressed little but disdain for the enemy, observing that the "Supreme Joy" of Britons "Seems to be Ravageing, fighting, and Shedding of blood." Appropriately enough for a young combat officer, Kirkwood felt that the only way to confront such aggression was with force of arms. Kirkwood concluded by reminding his fellow soldiers that "on your Beheavour Depends your future enjoyment of peace and liberty, or your Subjection to a Tyrannical Enemy, with all its Grieveous Consequences. When, therefore, you Come to Engage—think of your Ancestors—& think of your posterity."[18]

Peter Jaquett and Robert Kirkwood were nearly perfect contemporaries of the same age and disposition. For the armies of the Revolution, few men were as vital to maintaining unit cohesion than company-grade officers—ensigns, lieutenants and captains—who played a key role in transferring orders from higher up the chain of command. Junior officers were likewise expected to play a delicate balancing act. Very often drawn from the same communities as the men under their command, they were expected to foster an air of professional rapport with their men, but never at the expense of the appropriate mantle of authority that was so imperative to the preservation of discipline. Leading by personal example was the requisite duty for company-grade officers, who expected men to follow them into combat. "Remember," George Washington had instructed his junior officers in 1756, "that it is the actions, and not the Commission, that make the Officer and that there is more expected from him than the Title."[19]

Both Kirkwood and Jaquett fulfilled this role during the Revolutionary War. In the final years of the war during the Southern Campaign, they would transcend this role to assume far more responsibility in leading the Delaware Regiment despite their relatively modest military rank.

Peter Jaquett enlisted in Haslet's Delaware Regiment on January 1, 1776, and was commissioned in the Fourth Company as an ensign. Robert Kirkwood followed on January 17 with appointment as a first lieutenant. In August 1776, the Delaware Regiment, under Colonel John Haslet, marched to Philadelphia, where they were fully armed with recently imported muskets and bayonets. Captain Thomas Holland was appointed as adjutant. He had served with the British army and was able to make the Delaware Regiment one of the best-drilled and smartest units in the Continental army. Holland was to perish in the Battle of Germantown.[20]

Fully fitted out, the Delaware troops were described as "the best uniformed and equipped in the continental army of 1776." Wearing uniforms of blue coats faced and lined in red, each soldier also wore a white waistcoat. Buttons on privates' coats were pewter and on the officer's gilt, bearing the initials "DR" for Delaware Regiment. Their breeches were cotton (buckskin the year later), with white woolen stockings and black spatterdashes or gaiters. The hats of the troops were small, round black-jacked leather hats with a high peak front. On each hat inscribed in gilt was written "Liberty and Independence, Delaware Regiment" and ornamented with an image of "the Delaware Crest" with a depiction of a full-rigged ship and within a center scroll a sheaf of wheat. The color of their coats caused the troops to be popularly known first as the "Delaware Blues." When on parade, the men stuck short red feathers on the left side of their caps.[21] Their uniform served as a model for what would later be the uniform of all the Continental troops.

On August 8, 1776, the regiment was ordered to march to Amboy, New Jersey, and the impending contest to control New York City. Although not the first clash of the Revolution, this would be the first set-piece battle between

Opposite: A Plan of the Operations of the King's Army under the Command of General Sr. William Howe, K.B. in New York and East New Jersey, against the American Forces Commanded by General Washington, From the 12th of October. The map depicts the various campaigns of October and November 1776 in northern Manhattan, lower Westchester and East New Jersey. "It is the most accurate published delineation of the movements of the armies of Washington and Howe in Westchester, from the time of the British landing through November 28, particularly focusing on the Battle of White Plains." The British and Hessian troop landings in the areas of Mamaroneck, Larchmont, New Rochelle, Pelham Manor and the Bronx are clearly outlined. Also shown is Cornwallis's capture of Fort Lee and his pursuit of the American army through New Jersey that would end in Washington's crossing of the Delaware River. *Library of Congress.*

opponents on an open field in battle array. On arriving in Long Island, the Delaware Regiment was repeatedly referred to as the largest in camp.[22]

The Delaware Blues joined the Maryland battalion of General William Smallwood, which was even better armed and more dazzling in scarlet coats lined in buff.[23] These two organizations would be often joined throughout the remainder of the war.

BATTLE OF LONG ISLAND (NEW YORK, AUGUST 26–29, 1776)

Kirkwood and Jaquett received their baptism of fire at the Battle of Long Island, where the Delaware Regiment successfully covered Washington's retreat. Jaquett was subsequently promoted to lieutenant. After the British evacuation of Boston, Washington immediately moved his army, less the militia, to New York City, in anticipation of a British invasion of that strategically important city. During July and August 1776, General Howe, supported by a British fleet under his brother, Admiral Lord Richard Howe, landed an army of thirty-two thousand British and Hessian regulars unopposed on Staten Island. But by late August, Washington had assembled a force of more than twenty thousand virtually untrained Continentals and militia and built a system of defenses on and around Manhattan Island. About half of these colonial troops were deployed in fortifications on Brooklyn Heights and forward positions at the western end of Long Island under command of Major General Israel Putnam. From August 22 to August 25, General Howe landed about twenty thousand soldiers on Long Island and, in the evening of August 26, directed a wide flanking movement around the American left, commanded by Major General John Sullivan. On the morning of the following day, Howe fell on the rear of Sullivan's forces, and despite a valiant defense by the Continentals on the right under Brigadier General William Alexander (Lord Stirling), the whole American front crumpled. Enoch Anderson, a nineteen-year-old lieutenant of the Delaware Continentals, wrote, "A little before day, as we marched towards the enemy two miles from our camp we saw them." In no time at all, they were in the middle of a hot engagement.[24]

In their first battle, at Long Island on August 27, 1776, the men of Haslet's Delaware Blues won the praise of their commanders and the respect of the entire army for their gallant action, standing with Smallwood's First Maryland Regiment under Stirling's Brigade, allowing Washington to

Battle of Long Island. Retreat of the Americans under General Stirling across Gowanus Creek, 1860. *Library of Congress (LC-USZ62-39078).*

safely retreat with his forces intact. The Delaware men and the Maryland Regiment were to fight side by side throughout most of the war. The two forces typically deployed together, and the Delaware men were operationally under the command of the Marylanders.[25]

As the morning progressed, the enemy began to encircle the Americans. The only possible escape route was to cross under heavy fire a marshy area about eighty yards wide called Gowanus Creek. On the other side was the stronger American position of Brooklyn Heights. Lord Stirling ordered most of his men toward the Gowanus Creek, and about half the First Maryland Regiment and most of the First Delaware Regiment were able to retreat. Stirling stayed with about four hundred battle-weary Maryland and Delaware survivors to serve as a rear guard.

Two thousand British infantrymen and Hessians surrounded the Marylanders and Delawareans. Many of the British fired from the windows of a building known locally as the "Old Stone House." In the smoke and confusion of battle, the house must have looked like a fortress. Then Lord Stirling and the "Maryland 400" did the unexpected. They charged toward the Old Stone House with their muskets and bayonets.

According to survivor accounts, the British "infantry poured volleys of musket balls in almost solid sheets of lead" at the Marylanders and Delawareans. Forced to retreat, they regrouped over their dead and wounded friends and colleagues and charged a second time with their fixed bayonets. Then they did it a third time.

When the fighting was ended, 256 Marylanders and Delawareans lay dead on the ground in the vicinity of the Old Stone House, more than 60 percent of the attacking force and one of the largest fatality percentage rates for any battle in American history. More than 100 were captured, but many of those Marylanders and Delawareans died as prisoners of war. Only a few dozen of the "Maryland 400" escaped alive back to American lines.

The significance of the "Maryland 400" cannot be overstated. The intense fighting near the Old Stone House lasted almost an hour, which allowed many Americans to escape with their lives. More importantly, it halted the British offensive for the day, which otherwise might have led to the capture of General Washington and his army. The sacrifice of the "Maryland 400," although a more apt term would be the "Maryland and Delaware 400," quite possibly saved the Revolutionary War.[26]

In Long Island, they fought in the thickest of the fighting and held on to keep a defeat from turning into a disastrous rout. An eyewitness wrote that they had "sustained the hottest of the enemy's fire....They fought and fell like Romans."[27] Thirty-one Delawareans were killed, wounded or captured in the engagement. With great pride and no exaggeration, Colonel John Haslet would describe how his "Delawares" stood with "determined countenance," in close array, their colors flying, the enemy's artillery "playing" on them all the while and the enemy, "though six times their number," not daring to attack.[28]

Remnants of the forward American forces fled back to entrenchments on Brooklyn Heights and two nights later were evacuated to Manhattan in a skillful withdrawal unobserved by the British. Estimates place total American losses at 300 to 400 killed and wounded and 700 to 1,200 taken prisoners. General Howe listed his losses as 367.

WHITE PLAINS (NEW YORK, OCTOBER 25, 1776)

During its next major engagement at White Plains, the First Delaware Regiment once again demonstrated its valor. Haslet's Regiment had been reduced to 548 men, and of these only 273 were fit for duty. Along with a total Continental strength of some 1,600 American troops, they defended their hill position against an overpowering force of about 7,500 men. Haslet's men defended Chatterton's Hill, retreating only as the American forces did. When the American right flank was exposed, it was the New York, Maryland and Delaware regiments that took the brunt of 4,000 British troops and cavalry who had crossed the Bronx River to engage them. Haslet's men twice repelled light troops and horses of the enemy, but sheer numbers overwhelmed them as they were forced to withdraw. Among the Blue Hens, 15 were killed and 15 more wounded in the engagement.[29] A commentator wrote that "these so few slender…defended their position with coolness and tenacity."[30]

After the loss of Forts Washington and Lee in November, the American army withdrew from New York into New Jersey, with British troops in pursuit. The Delaware Blue Hens retreated with Washington southwest through New Jersey, pursued by the British to a defensive line across the Delaware River. Reflecting on their losses, Peter Jaquett of the Fourth Company of Haslet's Delaware Regiment wrote, "A thick cloud of darkness and gloom covered the land and despair was seen in almost every countenance."[31]

TRENTON (NEW JERSEY, DECEMBER 26, 1776)

The original term of enlistment for the "Delawares" expired in January, and many returned home. Suffering from defeat and desertion, Washington desperately needed a victory, or this fight would soon be over. He engineered a brilliant one at the Battle of Trenton.

The British had followed up their success on Long Island with a series of landings on Manhattan Island that compelled Washington to retire northward to avoid entrapment. When Forts Washington and Lee on the Hudson above Manhattan were lost in mid-November 1776, Washington retreated across New Jersey with General Howe in close pursuit, escaping finally over the Delaware into Pennsylvania with about three thousand men. Howe then went into winter quarters in New York City, leaving garrisons at Newport, Rhode Island, and in several New Jersey towns.

Washington determined to make a surprise attack on the British garrison in Trenton, a 1,400-man Hessian force, in the hope that a striking victory would lift the badly flagging American morale. Reinforcements had raised

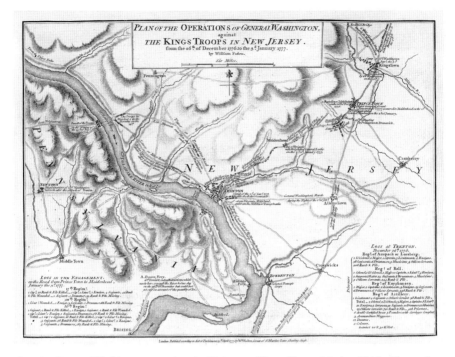

Opposite: George Washington crossing the Delaware River. Henry Mosler, 1912. *Library of Congress (LC-USZCN4-159).*

Above: *The King's Troops in New Jersey*, by William Faden. Plan of the operations of General Washington, against the king's troops in New Jersey, from December 26, 1776, to January 3, 1777. *Library of Congress.*

Washington's army to about 7,000, and on Christmas night (December 25–26), he ferried about 2,400 men of this force across the ice-choked Delaware in wet weather alternately raining, sleeting and snowing to surprise a Hessian force at Trenton. At 8:00 a.m., they converged on Trenton in two columns, achieving complete surprise. After only an hour and a half of fighting, the Hessians surrendered. Some 400 of the garrison escaped southward to Bordentown, New Jersey, when two other American columns failed to get across the Delaware in time to intercept them. About 30 were killed and 918 captured along with large quantities of stores. American losses were only 2 dead of exposure and 5 wounded in battle. Haslet's Delaware Regiment was among the last units to cross the Delaware River for the surprise attack on the Hessian camp at Trenton, New Jersey. The Delawareans were at the center of the American line (under Stirling), and after several volleys from American cannons, they charged down King and Queen Streets,

A nineteenth-century lithograph titled "Surrender of the Hessian troops to General Washington, after the Battle of Trenton, Decr. 25th 1776." *Anne S.K. Brown Military Collection.*

overwhelming all opposition. This victory renewed hope for the cause of independence. Some 92 soldiers of the Delaware Regiment participated in this successful raid.

PRINCETON (NEW JERSEY, JANUARY 3, 1777)

After the successful coup at Trenton, Washington recrossed the Delaware into Pennsylvania with his Hessian prisoners. He reoccupied Trenton on December 30–31, 1776, and collected there a force of 5,200 men, about half of whom were militia. Washington next moved on Princeton, where a large cache of British stores and arms were the prize. Meanwhile, Major General Charles Cornwallis, British commander in New Jersey, who was in New York at the time of the attack on Trenton, returned, gathering troops as he came. He entered Trenton with some 6,000 British regulars on January 2, 1777, and faced Washington's forces, which had withdrawn southward behind Assunpink Creek. The Americans were in a most precarious position with their backs to the Delaware River.

Fortunately, Cornwallis delayed his attack until the following morning. This gave Washington's men an opportunity to steal off quietly by a side road during the night of January 2–3, leaving their campfires burning brightly. They slipped southward and eastward, undetected, around the enemy's flank, and by the morning of January 3, they had arrived at Princeton, where they encountered a column of British regulars led by Colonel Charles Mawhood just leaving the town to join Cornwallis. On January 3, 1777, avoiding the main British forces at Trenton, the offensive drive faltered under a bayonet charge led by British lieutenant colonel Mawhood's troops. Mawhood overextended himself, became exposed to crossfire and barely escaped total entrapment, at the loss of four hundred casualties, including about one hundred killed. In a brief engagement, the Americans defeated the British, inflicting losses of four hundred to six hundred killed, wounded and prisoners at a cost of thirty Patriots killed and wounded. Mawhood's force retired in disorder toward Trenton and New Brunswick, while Washington moved on north to Morristown, where thickly wooded hills provided protection against a British attack. Here he established his winter headquarters on the flank of the British line of communications, compelling General Howe to withdraw his forces in New Jersey back to New Brunswick and points eastward.

Among the American casualties was the death of Colonel Haslet, who had led the Delaware Regiment since its original muster. Haslet had written to a friend, "I have had the piles and swollen legs.…But no matter if we drive them to New York. If I return it will be to salute you, if not we will meet in heaven."[32] Reduced to approximately one hundred men, the First Delaware Regiment was disbanded before the Battle of Princeton. Only Haslet, Dr. Tilton and a tiny handful of Delawareans remained for the Battle of Princeton.[33] The enlisted men's terms were expiring, and the officers were sent back to Delaware to recruit replacements. The First Delaware Regiment was disbanded before the Battle of Princeton on January 3, 1777.

Haslet's Regiment began its brief war as one of the largest and best-equipped units in Washington's host. But after five months of intense action and many casualties, it was a spent force.

The Delaware Regiment in the campaign of 1776 consisted of 42 officers and 768 rank and file. Of these, 4 officers, including the gallant commander, were killed and 16 wounded. Of the rank and file, many were killed or wounded, but many more died of the "camp fever."[34] More than half of the officers of Haslet's Regiment refused to serve in the next campaign. This was truly "a time that tried men's souls."

General George Washington rallying the troops at the Battle of Princeton, by William Ranney. *Princeton University Art Museum.*

Captains Kirkwood and Anderson were among the most prompt and successful at recruiting. By January 20, Kirkwood had enlisted seventy noncommissioned officers and privates. However, ten had deserted by the following month. Anderson tallied seventy-eight and lost eleven in the same period.

Peter Jaquett was promoted to captain on January 8, 1777.[35]

Chapter 3

COLONEL HALL'S
DELAWARE REGIMENT

*C*olonel David Hall's Delaware Regiment of the Continental Line fought the longest, until the cessation of hostilities in 1783. Many times during the war, it may have seemed like a forlorn cause. The Revolutionary cause was approaching a nadir, with losses at the Battle of Long Island and White Plains while retreating across New Jersey.

The Delaware Continentals were enlisted for the duration of the war and were promised a bounty of twenty dollars and one hundred acres of land to them or their survivors after the war. Nine of Haslet's original officers were attracted to the greater rewards and the opportunity for advancement and left Haslet's First Delaware for this new regiment along with a number of enlisted soldiers.[36]

RECRUITING AND FORMATION

Jaquett subsequently joined Hall's Delaware Regiment of the Continental Line as captain of the Fourth Company. He assisted Captain Kirkwood in recruiting a company and marched with them in February to Princeton and Brunswick. Captain Robert Kirkwood commanded the Second Company.[37]

Congress, grown tired of the difficulties driven by short terms of enlistment, reorganized the American army on September 16, 1776, to

Private
1781

Private, Light Company
1778

Captain

Private
1778

Colonel Hall's Delaware Regiment Continental Line, 1777–83, showing a private in buckskins; a private, Light Company; a captain; and another private. Kirkwood's Delawares were distinguished by the gold band on their cocked hats. *Delaware Military Museum.*

authorize the recruiting of eighty-eight battalions to serve for the *duration* of the war. Delaware was to raise one regiment or battalion of eight hundred men. The Committee of Safety of Delaware proceeded to raise its quota, and in four months the third Delaware regiment, under Colonel David Hall, joined Washington in New Jersey. This regiment became known as the Delaware Regiment of the Continental Line. It would serve for the duration of the war in many campaigns and battles, ending the war at Yorktown.

Its list of battle honors nearly constitutes a history of the Revolution itself. During seven years of service, the Delaware Regiment earned a staggering combat record at the most legendary engagements of the war, including Long Island, White Plains, Trenton, Brandywine, Germantown, Monmouth, Camden, Cowpens, Guilford Court House, Hobkirk's Hill, Ninety Six and Eutaw Springs. Its men were regarded as crack troops and regularly given the toughest assignments.

Kirkwood and Jaquett were among nine officers of Haslet's contingent who returned home in late 1776 to obtain commissions in a reconstituted Delaware battalion led by Captain David Hall, who became colonel of the regiment. Captain Charles Pope was appointed as lieutenant colonel, Captain Joseph Vaughn as its major, Lieutenant John Patten as captain of the first company, Lieutenant Robert Kirkwood as captain of the second company, Lieutenant John Learmouth as captain of the third company and Ensign Peter Jaquett as captain of the fourth company. Only sixteen of Haslett's forty-two officers gained a commission with Hall's regiment.

When fully organized, Hall's regiment, like Haslet's, comprised eight companies.[38] At the end of January, however, it could only muster two companies strong enough to deploy. The two companies led by Kirkwood and Jaquett joined the army at Princeton in March. Only in May did Colonel Hall arrive with the remaining companies, and the regiment topped out with only 312 soldiers. This "half-regiment" was assigned to a brigade with three Maryland regiments led by Colonel William Smallwood at Morristown, New Jersey.

We have a copy of a surviving letter from Captain Kirkwood to his father from this period. There must have been many such letters, but this is the only one to survive history. It is an illuminating snapshot of life in the Delaware Regiment. The letter describes the hardships and challenges of life on the march and Kirkwood's response. It is indicative of the kind of resourceful officer Kirkwood was. He frequently seized opportunity and eagerly (and entertainingly) took the initiative, as evidenced here:

Brunswick June 23rd, 1777
Hon'd Father

I have the pleasure of dating my letter from this place, which has of a long time been the den of thieves and murderers. I intend this letter as a Journal of what has happened since my last writing to you. By the time I sealed my last letter, our division were all under arms. We marched first to Kingston, and from thence to a place called Rocky hill, five miles south, west of Somerset Court House. At that place our whole division encamped for the night. Next morning we were alarmed by the firing of cannon and were immediately under arms. From thence we marched to Correll's ferry on the Delaware, with great precipitation, to secure our baggage on the other side of the river. When we had come in sight of the ferry we were ordered one and a half miles back, where we lay that night at the roots of trees, I was so tired, that I slept as sound as I ever did on a bed. The next morning being the 15th instant, we began our march back by the same road we came the day before, when we turned to the left and marched on until we came to a place called Sowerland Mountain, where we encamped and immediately set to building booths of birch. Just as I had completed one for myself, orders came to me, that I must command a picquet guard, about three miles from where we were encamped, which was not pleasing, as we had been three days constantly marching. But getting my guard ready I set off for the place which I was ordered. After marching about a mile, I stopped at a tavern where the Hon. Major general Sullivan was. I requested him to let me have a scouting party as a detachment of the picquet, and a guide to show me the road where the enemy lay. My request was granted, and with my guide I proceeded on my march. Upon coming to the place appointed, I stopped—took out fifty men for the scout, and left the same number behind.

I took Lieutenant Mohannon along with me and proceeded towards the enemy who lay about a mile and a half from our picquet. I told my guide if he deceived me, he should be the first I would Kill. He promised very fair, but said he did not know the very place where their out picquet lay. After marching the distance of a mile and a half from the picquet, as near as I could guess, I stopped at a house; it being then between the hours of ten and eleven at night. The People of the house seemed much frightened at my appearance among them at first, but when they found out who we were, they were satisfied. I inquired if we were near their sentries. I was told we were on the enemy's side of them, and that a wheat field I had passed seemed red with them at dark. I thought my situation none of the pleasantest and immediately withdrew a little distance from the house. My guide informed me, that a man who lived a mile from where we were was then among the regulars, but came home almost every night. That he had a negro man bound apprentice to him to learn the trade of weaving, and that the master of the negro offered a considerable sum to any person who would bring him his servant. It being the dead of night and my guide being timorous, I thought I would pass away some more of the night by trying if I could get the tory and the negro. Upon coming near the house I heard the door shut. I then divided my party into three divisions and surrounded the house. I left the men about three rods from the house and went in myself. The woman seemed much frightened. I asked her if there had been any rebels there lately. Finding that I was on that strain of the discourse, marks of joy appeared on her countenance and she answered—"Lord they have scarcely left the house, take care or they will surround you." I told her not to be under the least apprehension, for I thought I could nearly drive all the rebels myself. She replied, "You can't think how numerous they are."

She caused her daughter to bring me sweet milk to drink and bread and butter to eat; and sent out a cheese to the men, and divided two loaves of bread among them. She then asked me, "If I had seen her husband lately?" I told her I had not, but believed he lay in the centre division between Brunswick and Somerset. She begged me, for heaven's sake, not to let him come out any more, or he would be taken by the rebels, for that they were hourly after him. I promised to comply with her wishes, and told her, her husband understood my intention of coming out his evening, and requested the favor of me to bring him a negro who that was bound to him. She answered that she would send him with all her heart, but the boy being scared that evening had gone to a house about three miles off. I asked if it were a plain road. She said, "No, it is very difficult." Seeing a little boy, a son of hers about twelve years old, I told her if she would let him come along with me, I would do her husband the favor of getting his boy for him. At first she was afraid of our meeting the rebels, but on telling her of my numbers were very large, she consented to let her son go. I left the house holding the boy's hand in mine, and we soon got extremely sociable. He told me the rebels that day had taken all his father's horses, but one fine horse, his father had got at Brunswick last Winter, and for fear of the rebels, he had him sent to the house we were going to. He said that Mr. Gower (the name of the man whose house we were going) and his father were very great; that Glower [sic] was almost every day at General Washington's Camp to get news, and that he told his father all he could learn, as to the detached posts of the rebels, and their numbers at all different stations, and that his father told the regulars. I assure you the little boy knew as much of our army as I did.

Coming up to the house, I knocked at the door. Gower rose and let me in. I inquired whether the rebels had been there lately or not. He said they had been within sight that evening, but had not called. I told him, it being so fine a moonlit night, I could not think of returning without harassing them a little. He said my best way would be to lie by until daybreak at which time they would go down the road, and I would have a good opportunity of taking some of them prisoners as I was then within a half mile of the right regulars front division. I inquired for the negro boy, but he told me the rebels had taken him about dark. After I got all the intelligence I wanted from him, I made myself known; at which he was so struck that he could not speak a word. I then made him put on his clothes—sent for the horse I have mentioned, took his negro man and put both of them under guard, and so returned. Day broke by the time we had got within half a mile of our picquet.

From thence I sent Gower to the General, who had him ironed and sent to Flemington, and I have neither heard of tory, negro or horse since. His neighbors seemed very glad he was taken, for they said he was the very worst they had there. I returned in the morning by the way of the enemy's picquets, but found they had been called in the evening before the main body. So I went back to the mountains where we staid until the 19th instant. (On this day, the enemy set a number of houses on fire). We now marched back to Rocky hill, where we remained until the 22nd, and then marched to this place. The enemy left the bridge (which is a fine piece of work) standing. It is twelve feet wide, and has about thirty pillars.

We are now under marching orders, I suppose towards Amboy. It seems a little strange on the Sabbath day we should leave this place, and on the Sabbath day come into it again.

No more but remain your loving son,
ROBERT KIRKWOOD CAPT. D.R.[39]

Chapter 4

HOWE'S CHESAPEAKE INVASION

ritish commander General William Howe was repulsed at Trenton in his attempt to take Philadelphia. The campaign to seize Philadelphia, the second major phase of British strategy in 1777, began in late July. He outflanked Washington by embarking his sixteen-thousand-man army from New York on July 23, 1777, aboard a fleet of more than 260 vessels and sailing up the Chesapeake Bay avoiding the well-defended Delaware Bay and River. He landed with sixteen thousand soldiers at Head of Elk on August 25. This eighteenth-century amphibious landing, the D-Day of its time, must have been an impressive sight. Howe landed in two locations on Elk Neck Peninsula and marched one division through Elkton, Maryland, and the other crossed the Elk River east toward Middletown, turning north near what is now Lum's Pond, Delaware. The two forces joined at Aikentown (Glasgow) before moving northeast.[40]

Howe generously offered "a free and general pardon to all such officers and private men as shall voluntarily surrender themselves to any detachment of his majesty's forces."[41] There are no recorded takers to his offer. Washington's response was a promise of thirty-nine lashes "if any soldier shall dare to quit his ranks."[42]

Washington posted his army to positions around the present-day Marshallton-Stanton area on the banks of the Red Clay Creek. He selected a chosen force of some 720 men from every unit to serve as pickets and skirmishers to take up positions in the woods above Glasgow. They were

General Sir William Howe, the 5th Viscount Howe, commander of British land forces in the colonies, engraving by Henry Bryan Hall. *Wikimedia Commons.*

commanded by William Maxwell. "Give them as much trouble as you possibly can," instructed Washington.

Washington himself, along with his nineteen-year-old major general and aide Lafayette, reconnoitered the area on August 26, scouting Iron Hill and Gray's Hill only six miles from the British main camp. That evening, they sought shelter from a summer thunderstorm. Drenched, they spent the night at the home of an unnamed farmer at the foot of Chestnut Hill near Welsh Tract Church:

To The President of Congress
Wilmington, August 27, 1777.

Sir: I this Morning returned from the Head of Elk, which I left last night. In respect to the Enemy, I have nothing new to communicate, they remain where they debarked first. I could not find out from inquiry what number is landed, nor form an estimate of it, from the distant view I had of their Encampment. But few Tents were to be seen from Iron Hill and Grey's Hill, which are the only Eminences about Elk. I am happy to inform you, that all the Public Stores are removed from thence, except about Seven thousand Bushels of Corn. This I urged the Commissary there to get off, as soon as possible, and hope it will be effected in the course of the few days if the Enemy should not prevent, which their Situation gives them but too easy an opportunity of doing; The scarcity of Teams, in proportion to the demand, will render the removal rather tedious, though I have directed the Quarter Master to send some from hence, to expedite the Measure. A part of the Delaware Militia are Stationed there and about nine hundred more from Pennsylvania are now on the March [that way]. I also intended to move part of the Army that way today, but am under the necessity of defering it, till their Arms are put in order and they are furnished with Ammunition, both having been greatly injured by the heavy rain that fell yesterday and last night. I have the Honor etc. [43]

Geo. Washington

Cooch's Bridge (Delaware)

On September 3, the British Division, commanded by Lord Cornwallis, marched to Aikin's Tavern (Glasgow). In the van were Hessians under General Knyphausen. They were to advance some two miles to Cooch's Mill, cross the Christina and take up positions beyond. Concurrently, the Second Battalion of British light infantry had been sent to the right across the Christina Creek to attempt an attack on the American left and rear.

This locally famous clash included Delawareans of the militia but not of the Continentals. The Second New Castle County (Whig) Battalion, led by Colonel Samuel Patterson (who earlier had commanded the Delaware Flying Wing Regiment), had eight companies. In August 1777, the

NEWARK, DEL. COOCH'S BRIDGE. FLAG FIRST UNFURLED IN BATTLE 1777.   E. B. Frazer, Newark, Del.

Printed in Germany.

Cooch's Bridge Monument, Newark, Delaware, postcard dated 1905. *Newark Historical Society.*

Second New Castle County Battalion was assigned to Maxwell's Brigade of Light Infantry in the Continental army. The First New Castle County Battalion may have also served as a scouting force during the skirmish at Cooch's Bridge.

A force of seven hundred Delaware and nine hundred Maryland Light Infantry, along with nine hundred Philadelphia Light Horse commanded by General Maxwell, engaged a body of British troops at Cooch's Bridge on September 3, 1777. It was a fine weather day, cool early, turning excessively hot by afternoon.

That Second Battalion British Light Infantry went too deep and took itself out of play. Blocked from action by Purgatory Swamp, the battalion gave up its attempt at flanking and doubled back to assist the British troops engaged with Maxwell's at the bridge. When the British Second arrived back at the bridge, it found Maxwell's corps in orderly retreat.

A hot battle began on the road skirting Iron Hill as the forces met near present-day Route 896. Howe attempted to outflank and surround the smaller American force but was hemmed in by Iron Hill on one side and Purgatory Swamp on his right. The Americans made an especially strong stand at the site of Cooch's Bridge, which gives its name to this engagement, but were finally forced to retreat. Fighting continued up to Welsh Tract Meetinghouse before hostilities were broken off.

This sharp skirmish resulted in some forty American casualties. It was the only significant engagement of the war fought on Delaware soil. Local lore has it that the Stars and Stripes were unfurled in battle for the first time at Cooch's Bridge. Washington's army carried the flag for the first time in a parade through Philadelphia on July 24. This battle would be the first "firefight" between the two armies subsequently, and it would be entirely appropriate for the colors to be carried into a battle in this manner, although there is no specific evidence in the record.[44]

Because it was the only battle of the Revolution fought on Delaware soil, we offer General Washington's report to Congress:

> *Wilmington, 8 P.M. 3 of Sept. 1777. This morning the enemy came out with a considerable force and three pieces of artillery against our light advanced corps and after some pretty smart skirmishing obliged them to retreat being far superior in numbers and without cannon. The loss on either side is not yet ascertained, ours, though not exactly known, is not very considerable; theirs we have reason to believe, was much greater as some of our parties composed of expert marksmen had opportunity of giving them close, well directed fires, more particularly in one instance, when a body of riflemen formed a kind of ambuscade. They advanced about two miles this side of Iron Hill and then withdrew to that place, leaving a picket at Cooch's Mill about a mile in front. Our parties now lie at White Clay Creek, except the advance pickets which are at Christiana Bridge. The design of their movement this morning seems to have been to dispense our light troops, who had been troublesome to them, and to gain possession of Iron Hill; to establish a post there most probably for covering their retreat in case of accidents.*[45]

Washington withdrew, and the British encamped in the area for three days, September 3–6. The British burned down Thomas Cooch's barn and used Cooch's home as their headquarters. The war had come to Delaware. During September and October, the British occupied Wilmington. The Queen's Rangers, a Scots regiment, and some companies of Hessians garrisoned the town. The British captured Delaware's president (equivalent to governor at the time), John McKinly, and seized many public records. McKinly was exchanged after a year's imprisonment for Loyalist New Jersey Royal governor William Franklin, the son of Benjamin Franklin. From the autumn of 1777 through June 1778, the British purchased supplies in New Castle and Port Penn. In December, after the British withdrawal, General Washington ordered American forces back to the town. Smallwood's division of two brigades of Marylanders and Hall's Delaware Regiment took up quarters there.[46]

Brandywine (Pennsylvania, September 11, 1777)

Howe's forces then moved in three divisions through Newark and Kennett Square, Pennsylvania. Howe avoided the American entrenchments, keeping to the west of their strong points. He marched through Newark and Kennett Square and thence to Chad's Ford (now known as Chadd's Ford). Washington had expected them to move on Christiana and Wilmington. Washington moved from Newport along Center Road to Lancaster Pike to the Crooked Billet Tavern and then up Kennett Road. He kept his army between Howe and Philadelphia and took up positions near Chad's Ford, Pennsylvania, setting the stage for the next battle at Brandywine.

Washington, with about eleven thousand men, took up a defensive position blocking the way to Philadelphia at Chad's Ford on the eastern side of Brandywine Creek in Pennsylvania. The Delaware Regiment of

Opposite: Battle of the Brandywine. "Many of the Americans were unskilled militia but they repelled charge after charge of the infantry, chasseurs and grenadiers." By F.C. Yohn. *Library of Congress (LC-USZ62-100726)*.

Right: The Honorable Marquis Lafayette, major general of the American army. *Library of Congress (LC-USZ62-45239)*.

The Hon. MARQUIS LAFAYETTE,
Major General of the American Army.

the Continental Line was attached to a body of troops commanded by General Sullivan at the Battle of the Brandywine. Howe attacked on September 11, sending Cornwallis across the creek in a wide-sweeping flanking movement around the American right, while his Hessian troops demonstrated opposite Chad's Ford. Major General Nathanael Greene's troops staved off Cornwallis's threatened envelopment of Washington's whole force, and the Americans fell back to Chester in a hard-pressed but orderly retreat. Patriot losses in this engagement totaled about one thousand killed, wounded and prisoners. British casualties were fewer than six hundred, including ninety-three killed. More troops fought at Brandywine than any other battle of the American Revolution. It was also the second-longest single-day battle of the war, after the Battle of Monmouth, with continuous fighting for eleven hours.

According to Elizabeth Montgomery in *Reminiscences of Wilmington*, at the Battle of the Brandywine, Captain Jaquett told her that he was near Lafayette when he fell and heard him call to Washington, "General, I am wounded." The general, riding up, expressed his sorrow, and Lafayette replied, "Sir, I am not sorry."[47] The Delaware Regiment had been assigned to Stirling as a reserve in the center. When they were unexpectedly attacked, they made an orderly withdrawal. It is doubtful that this is a true account, as Lafayette and the Delaware Regiment were in disparate parts of the battlefield.

After the battle, Robert Kirkwood recorded in his order book, "Friday 19th returned back to our last encampment (Yellow Springs) being twelve miles, filed off to the left and forded Schuylkill (at Parkers's Ford) seven miles and halted in the woods at ten o'clock at night (then) marched through the trap (Trappe) to Richardson's ford being ten miles (in all 29 miles)."

Germantown (Pennsylvania, October 3–4, 1777)

After their victory at Brandywine, the British forces under Howe maneuvered in the vicinity of Philadelphia for two weeks, virtually annihilating a rear-guard force under Brigadier General Anthony Wayne at Paoli on September 21, 1777, before moving unopposed into the city on September 26. Howe established his main encampment in nearby Germantown, stationing some nine thousand men there. Washington promptly attempted a coordinated attack against this garrison on the night of October 3–4. Columns were to move into Germantown from four different directions and begin the assault at dawn. Two of the columns failed to take part in the attack, but in the early phases of the fighting, the columns under Greene and Wayne achieved considerable success. However, a dense early morning fog, which resulted in some American troops firing on one another while permitting the better-disciplined British to re-form for a counterattack, and a shortage of ammunition contributed to the still not fully explained retreat of the Americans, beginning about 9:00 a.m. Howe pursued the colonials a few miles as they fell back in disorder, but he did not exploit his victory.

The Delaware Regiment was in the thick of it, but Colonel Hall was wounded and would never lead the regiment again—nor would the regimental adjutant captain, Thomas Holland, also injured. American losses were 673 killed and wounded and about 400 taken prisoner. British losses were approximately 533 killed and wounded.

The Battle of Germantown (Chew's House), October 1777. *Library of Congress (LC-USZ62-56163).*

After his defeat at Germantown, Washington withdrew his forces to Valley Forge to go into winter camp. Washington again asked for the recruitment of additional troops from Delaware. The General Assembly made provision for enlisting 420 men. In May 1778, three companies of militia, one from each county, were raised to prevent enemy soldiers and refugees from landing in Delaware.

The year 1778 saw the American army ending its winter encampment at Valley Forge with a new sense of discipline and purpose; the British evacuated Philadelphia, shifting their focus to the south.

Monmouth (New Jersey, June 28, 1778)

After the conclusion of the Franco-American Alliance on February 6, 1778, British forces in America had to consider the new threat created by the powerful French fleet. General Clinton, who relieved Howe as British commander in America on May 8, 1778, decided to shift the main body of his troops from Philadelphia to a point nearer the coast, where it would be easier to maintain close communications with the British

General Washington at the Battle of Monmouth, circa 1856. *Library of Congress (LC-USZ62-7391).*

fleet. Consequently, he ordered evacuation of the 10,000-man garrison in Philadelphia on June 18. As these troops set out through New Jersey toward New York, Washington broke camp at his winter headquarters in Valley Forge and began pursuit of Clinton with an army of about 13,500 men, including the Delaware Blues. Advance elements under Major General Charles Lee launched the initial attack on the British column as it marched out of Monmouth Courthouse (now Freehold), New Jersey, on June 28, an extremely hot day.

For reasons not entirely clear, Lee did not follow up early advantages gained, and when British reinforcements arrived on the scene, he ordered a retreat. This encouraged Clinton to attack with his main force. Washington relieved Lee and assumed personal direction of the battle, which continued until dark without either side retiring from the field. But during the night, the British slipped away to Sandy Hook, New Jersey, from where their fleet took them to New York City. The British reported losses of 65 killed, 155 wounded and 64 missing; the Americans listed 69 killed, 161 wounded and 130 missing. The Delawares were held in reserve and suffered no casualties. General Lee was subsequently court-martialed and suspended from service for disobedience and misbehavior. Washington's army moved northward, crossed the Hudson and occupied positions at White Plains, New York.

There were no significant military operations in the north during the winter of 1778 or in the spring of 1779. On May 12, 1779, the Delaware Regiment was reorganized into nine companies and assigned to the Second Maryland Brigade under Colonel William Gist and Major General Johann de Kalb.

STONY POINT (NEW YORK, JULY 16, 1779)

In a well-planned and well-executed nighttime attack, a select, highly trained group of George Washington's Continental army troops under the command of General "Mad Anthony" Wayne defeated British troops in a quick and daring assault on their outpost in Stony Point, New York, approximately thirty miles north of New York City. Allen McLane had reconnoitered the position the day before. The British suffered heavy losses in a battle that served as a huge victory in terms of morale for the Continental army. While the fort was ordered evacuated quickly after the battle by General Washington, this key crossing site was used later in the war by units of the Continental army to cross the Hudson River on their way to victory over the British.

PAULUS HOOK (NEW JERSEY, AUGUST 19, 1779)

The Delaware Regiment of the Continental Line, the "Delaware Blues," continued its service. The regiment participated in the Battles of Stony Point and Paulus Hook in the summer of 1779. The Battle of Paulus Hook was between Continental army and British forces. The Patriots were led by

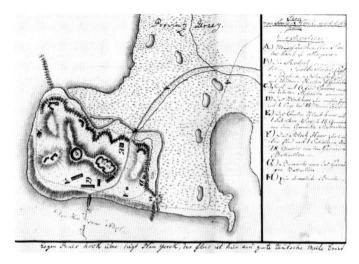

Paulus Hook Fort (1776–83), a Patriot fortification established in 1776 in present-day Jersey City, Hudson County, New Jersey. Named Paulus Hook Fort after the location, it was captured by the British in 1776 and held by them until 1783. It returned to Patriot control in 1783 just prior to the British evacuation of New York City. It was abandoned as a fortification in 1783 at the end of the war. *FortWiki.com.*

Major Henry "Light-Horse Harry" Lee and launched a nighttime raid on the British-controlled fort in what is today downtown Jersey City. They surprised the British, taking 158 prisoners, and withdrew with the approach of daylight. Despite retaining the fort and its cannons, the British lost much of their control over New Jersey. The Blues saw little action the remainder of 1779, and they wintered at Morristown, New Jersey.

In the spring of 1780, General Washington was assembling a force to attempt to dislodge the British from New York with the help of the French fleet and troops under the command of French general Rochambeau. As the First Delaware Regiment of the Continental Line had already sailed south from Elkton on May 8 to fight in the Southern Campaign, a request for more troops was issued to the Delaware Assembly in July 1780.

Linking Colonel Haslet and Kirkwood, the author Christopher Ward said, "It is not too much to say that no regimental officers in the whole army have more excellent records or achieved greater distinction than these two soldiers of Delaware. The universal recognition of their soldiership accorded them by their comrades in arms, by contemporary writers and all historians of the war is sure proof of that."[48]

Ward's words could equally apply to Peter Jaquett. He was literally at Kirkwood's side for the entire war. He and Kirkwood were the regiment's longest-serving captains. In the narrative accompanying his request for military pension, Jaquett wrote, "I served in the Delaware Regiment from the beginning to the end of the Revolutionary War with Captain Robert Kirkwood, each of our commissions were dated January 4, 1776 and I believe that neither one of us were ever absent from our Regiment without leave."[49]

Chapter 5

THE SOUTHERN CAMPAIGN

After 1778, the main theater of war shifted to the South as the British concentrated on trying to reestablish their control of that area. In the final years of the war, following the fall of Charleston to the British in May 1780, the South became the principal theater of the Revolutionary War. In addition to regular fighting between the armies, a civil war erupted between Patriots and Loyalists, with many small battles between militias raging throughout the countryside.

By 1781, the British were convinced that control could not be accomplished while Virginia continued to serve as a base for American military operations. Washington could ill-afford to strip his command of troops as New York remained occupied by Clinton and was an easy match for the ten thousand American troops opposing him.

Following the American surrender at Charleston on May 12, 1780, the Continental army's Southern Department was in disarray. Taken prisoner that day were 245 officers and 2,326 enlisted, including Major General Benjamin Lincoln, the Southern Department's commander-in-chief, along with militia and armed citizens, the most American prisoners surrendered at one time during the American Revolution.[50]

All Washington could spare from the Continental army were the Maryland and Delaware Regiments, consisting of some 2,000 soldiers in total, augmented by a Virginia artillery regiment with twelve artillery pieces. The Delaware Regiment was led by Lieutenant Colonel Joseph Vaughan. On April 16, 1780, about 1,400 soldiers broke camp at Morristown, New

Jersey, and marched to Head of Elk to be transported to Richmond and Petersburg on May 3 in order to assemble for the march south.[51] These troops were under the command of Major General Baron de Kalb. These forces were to be reinforced by Virginia and North Carolina militia and supported by those states with funds, ammunition and supplies.[52] Lieutenant Thomas Anderson recorded in his diary, "[May] 8th Set sail from the Head of Elk in company with fifty sail of vessels, being the Second Maryland Brigade, destined for Petersburg, in Virginia, at which place the sloop I was in arrived on the 23d, sailing in all, 350 [miles]."[53]

This logistic support failed to materialize in quantities sufficient to meet the needs of this expeditionary force. The result was many delays and a defensive posture as the army slowly advanced through an inhospitable terrain of lightly settled swamps and woods devoid of food and fodder at this time of year. It was not until June that the force had moved from Virginia to North Carolina at Hillsborough.

The troops faced a British force of Redcoats and Loyalist militia headquartered in Charleston under General Lord Cornwallis. He had about 8,500 men in his expeditionary force, well supported with artillery, stores and provisions. Cornwallis could count seven battalions of Loyalist militia numbering 4,000 men.

The Patriot situation came to the attention of Congress, which appointed General Gates commander of the force. General Horatio Gates was the victor over Burgoyne at the Battle of Saratoga and was a controversial rival to General George Washington, whom he had tried to discredit and had attempted to replace. By 1780, Gates was well known for personality conflicts with his fellow officers, prominently Benedict Arnold and Washington. But Gates's political reputation, at least, had survived his conflict with Washington, and he was still well regarded for his rapport with the enlisted and volunteer militia. Gates's Congressional appointment on June 4 was made without the council of General Washington. Washington had favored his ablest general, Nathanael Greene.[54]

Gates arrived in late July to assume overall command from de Kalb, who remained as commander of the Maryland and Delaware Regiments. Gates's orders "to march at a moment's warning" was a matter of great astonishment to those who knew the real situation of the troops. The countryside was "by nature barren, abounding with sandy plains, intersected by swamps, and very thinly inhabited," with a population hostile to the American cause, while the route through Charlotte was "in the midst of a fertile country and inhabited by a people zealous in the cause of America."[55]

General Horatio Gates, by Gilbert Stuart. *Metropolitan Museum of Art.*

These soldiers had few uniforms or proper kit, but they all proudly wore a green sprig in their hats and bore their firelock "with an air of skillful training." They were a battle-tested troop of seasoned veterans by this stage of the war.

North Carolina was rough country, with few roads and bridges but many swamps and trees. The men were supported by few supplies and were forced

Map of the Providence of South Carolina in North America, circa 1779. Library of Congress (LC-USZ62-29191).

to live off the countryside, poor as it was. Sergeant Major William Seymour of the Delaware Regiment recorded:

> At this time, we were very much distressed for want of provisions, insomuch that we were obliged to send our parties through the country, to thrash out grain for our sustenance; and this availed not much, for what was procured after this manner could scarce keep the troops from starving, which occasioned a vast number of men to desert to the enemy. Sometimes we drew half a pound of beef per man, and that so miserably poor that scarce any mortal could make use of it—living chiefly on green apples and peaches.[56]

They had little tentage and were forced to take shoes from their enemy casualties. Their condition was described as "truly miserable, weak and sickly." One result was an epidemic of desertions. General Gates wrote to Governor Thomas Jefferson of Virginia, "Flour, rum and droves of bullocks should without delay be forwarded to this Army or the Southern Department will soon want one to defend it." These pleas went unanswered.

The local Carolina militia had swept the field clean of any provisions that might find their way to the Continentals. Green corn was cooked with lean, stringy beef from the swamps and woods. Green peaches were substituted for bread, with distressing consequences. Rum was lacking, and molasses was used as a substitute. The molasses turned out to have been spoiled, causing diarrhea. The intestinal troubles suffered by the troops as a result of this poor diet resulted in sickness and disease that reduced the numbers of able-bodied.

Disease and Illness

Military leaders on both sides recognized the perils of warm weather campaigning in the feverish Lowcountry of the Carolinas and Georgia. More soldiers died from illness and disease than on the battlefield during the Revolutionary War. Sick soldiers who were unable to perform their duties created a problem for any army set to do battle. Widespread illness could hinder their movement as well as their strategies. Smallpox was rampant in the colonial era and killed millions before inoculation became common in the mid-eighteenth century. The disease, which has a ten- to fourteen-day incubation period, included symptoms like fever, headache, severe fatigue and back pain. Small red spots would appear on the skin and turn into fluid-filled blisters that eventually became pus. Once the lesions dried up and fell off, deep-pitted scars were often left on the skin.

Smallpox outbreaks had a large impact throughout the Revolutionary War, but the bigger threat was "camp fever," which is believed to be typhus. Typhus is a deadly bacterial infection transmitted by fleas, ticks and lice. It was known to spread rapidly throughout the overcrowded, unhygienic army camps. Early symptoms of typhus are similar to those of other illnesses, including fever, headache, body aches, cough and diarrhea.

Dysentery was also a problem in army camps during this time. Early in the war, Continental army encampments weren't yet up to the standards of European armies. For instance, the latrines were often too close to the camp itself.

It was the British who suffered the most significant losses from the region's fevers, however, particularly during the campaign of 1780. It began well, with Sir Henry Clinton's capture of Charleston in May. Yet Clinton's southern strategy seriously undermined the health of his forces and may have cost the British the war. To secure control over the lower South required keeping thousands of their soldiers in what was then the unhealthiest region of British North America. Malaria and other fevers killed and incapacitated large numbers of soldiers and felled key officers and commanders at critical moments. Despite winning another key victory at Camden, British forces in the region sustained heavy casualties from disease in the summer and fall of 1780. A few days after the battle, Cornwallis informed Clinton that his army's "sickness was very great, and truly alarming." His officers were especially hard-hit, and the head surgeon and almost all of his assistants were ill: "Every member of my family, and every public officer is now incapable of doing his duty."[57]

Camden (South Carolina, August 13, 1780)

At the Battle of Camden, the Delaware Blues and troops from Maryland saved the Continental army from complete destruction. On August 13, as Seymour wrote, the army was joined by some three thousand men from Virginia and the Carolinas, which seemed a good omen of success but instead proved to be

> *our utter ruin in the end, for, placing too much confidence in them, they at length deceived us and left us in the lurch. We marched...the baggage following close in the rear so confident was the General, and indeed it was everyone's opinion, that we should drive the enemy, we being far superior to them in numbers, we having three thousand militia and about 1,300 standing troops, and they not exceeding thirteen hundred here.*[58]

Gates's force began to advance toward the enemy at 8:00 p.m. on a very warm and muggy evening. Even during the advance, the men had to frequently stop to evacuate their bowels as a result of the spoiled molasses they had consumed. The van of the two armies met to "very hot fire" in the dim light of night at 2:30 a.m. on a battlefield flanked by two swamps about 1,200 yards apart. The Americans were on slightly higher ground and

Battle of Camden and the death of de Kalb, painted by Alonzo Chappel, 1857. *Library of Congress (LC-USZ62-11210).*

arranged in four groups. On the left were Continental veterans, 280 men of the Delaware Regiment and 350 men of the Second Maryland Brigade. In the center were 1,600 militia from North Carolina. On the right were 700 militia backed by 120 dragoons (mounted infantry) from Virginia. Behind the center were the 350 men of the First Maryland Brigade, held as a ready reserve. General Gates's command post was behind this, and the 170 wagons of the baggage train were in the rear.[59]

Facing the 2,300 colonial militiamen and 120 mounted infantry were British colonel James Webster's 600 experienced light infantry and 500 Irish volunteers, backed by Lieutenant Colonel Banastre Tarleton's 200 cavalry. Facing the 630 Continentals (backed by the 350 Continental reserve) were General Francis Rawdon's 500 infantry and a reserve of 400 Loyalist North Carolina militia. By 4:30 a.m., the two armies were in sight of each other in the early morning summer light.

At the start of the battle, both the British and American forces advanced. The Virginia militia, who had never before seen battle, faced experienced British troops, including light infantry. As the British charged, this militia panicked and fled into the woods. Most of the North Carolina militia similarly broke and fled through the First Maryland Brigade, pursued by the British cavalry. Many in the militia abandoned their muskets so as to run faster. At this point, General Gates mounted a fast horse and fled the field—a shameful action for which he was later removed from command. Colonel Smallwood of Maryland also abandoned the field of battle at this point, leaving the reserves without senior leadership. Otho Holland Williams estimated that two thousand of the three thousand Americans fled without firing a shot.

The British troops rolled up the flank of the regiment of North Carolina militia who had not fled and cut them off from the Continentals, killing one hundred and capturing several hundred more. The British cavalry swept on past the fray and captured the entire baggage and ammunition train (a total of 170 wagons) and then returned to the field and attacked the reserve troops. Lieutenant Thomas Anderson's journal records:

About one o'clock in the morning met with the enemy at Sutton's farm and drove back their advance guard. We then halted and formed the Line of battle, and lay on our arms until daylight, at which time the enemy advanced and charged our left wing, where the Militia was formed, who gave way, which give the enemy an opportunity of turning our left flank and got in our rear. The action soon became desperate and bloody for some time, but we were at last obliged to give way, with the loss of all our Artillery and baggage, and The loss of our Regiment in the action was Lieutenant Colonel Vaughan, Major Patten, Captains Learmonth and Rhodes, Lieutenants Purvis Duff Skilington and Roche, with seventy rank and file.[60]

On the left, the Delaware Blues and the Marylanders along with the North Carolinian regiment felt the whole brunt of the battle, and "nobly they sustained it." Major McGill, an aide to the commanding general, wrote in a letter after the battle, "We owe all misfortune to the militia, had they not run like dastardly cowards our army was sufficient to cope with them, drawn up as we were upon a rising and advantageous ground."[61]

Attacked in the front and on their flank, the Delaware Blues answered with a bayonet charge and took fifty prisoners. Outnumbered, they had to give ground but nevertheless regained it. Again driven back, they rallied once more and retook their old position. "Never, did troops show greater courage than these men of Maryland and Delaware." "No men," said Henry Cabot Lodge, "could have fought better than these soldiers."[62] On October 12, General Mordecai Gist wrote to Delaware governor Caesar Rodney:

> *I have the pleasure to inform you that the Officers and men of this Regiment, with the whole of the Regular Troops behav'd with the firmness and Intrepidity which would have ensured us a Compleat Victory, had not the scandalous conduct of the Militia, left us to oppose the Torrent of superior numbers....The loss of Men will render it necessary to reduce the Brigade and incorporate the whole into one Regiment, of which your Troops will form two Companies.*[63]

Nearly surrounded by advancing Crown forces, the Delaware Regiment lost about a third of its men during the fighting, many of them captured, including Lieutenant Colonel James Vaughan and Major John Patten and six other officers. In addition, it lost all its cannons and baggage to the enemy. A number of men in the regiment scattered during the confusion of the rout; Kirkwood and a handful of remaining fellow officers organized a breakout with about sixty Continentals.[64] Writing in his journal that evening, an exhausted Kirkwood simply referred to the fighting as "very Desparate."

General Gates was removed from command later that year after the disastrous Battle of Camden. Gates's military reputation was destroyed by the battle, and he did not hold another command for the remainder of the war. He was replaced by General Nathanael Greene in December 1780.

The Delaware Regiment was nearly annihilated. This had been its finest hour but also its darkest hour. It was truly the watershed battle of the war for the Delaware Regiment and for Captains Jaquett and Kirkwood. Out of 500 men who went into battle, only 188 remained alive and free. It had been the worst defeat suffered by the American army during the Revolutionary War.

Captain Robert Kirkwood took command of the pitiful remnant.[65] Without provision or supplies, the men marched 123 miles in five days to rejoin the army.

About 50 percent of the Continentals and 13 percent of the American militia were either killed or captured, compared with only 4 percent of the British troops. About 20 percent of the Delaware Regiment (fifty men) were killed, and 30 percent (seventy-two men) were taken prisoner, including six of the officers—Lieutenant Colonel Vaughan, Major Patten, Captains Rhodes and Learmouth and Lieutenants Duff and Purvis—and sixty-six soldiers.[66]

It took several weeks before the lost and demoralized men were once again collected into fighting units. Although half of those who had been taken prisoner were recaptured four days later, the Delaware Regiment was so decimated that it was reformed into two companies (under Captains Kirkwood and Jaquett) and merged into the Maryland Regiment for the rest of the war.

Baron Johann de Kalb

Baron Johann de Kalb was assigned to command a division of Maryland and Delaware troops in the Carolinas during the Southern Campaign.[67]

Jaquett's 1834 obituary notes, "At the disastrous battle of Camden, Baron Johann de Kalb while standing a little in advance of the Delaware regiment, had his horse shot under him, and as he lay endeavoring to extricate himself, a British horseman rushed upon him and upon the point of putting the gallant veteran to the sword, when Jaquett sprung from the line, drove his spontoon (pike) through the Englishman, in sight of both armies, secured his horse and placed the Baron upon it. At this moment de Kalb received a fatal wound and fell into the arms of Jaquett. To whom his last words were expressive of gratitude and admiration for his daring conduct."[68]

This may have been the embellished memory of an old soldier, recorded by a writer with no access to the factual record. In fact, de Kalb sustained eleven wounds and survived three days in British captivity, attended to by his aide-de-camp and friend Chevalier du Buysson.

Another account from Christopher Ward relates:

> De Kalb's horse was shot from under him. "Long after the battle was lost in every other quarter, the gigantic form of de Kalb, unhorsed and fighting on foot, was seen directing the movements of his brave Maryland and Delaware troops." His head had been laid open by a sabre-stroke, Captain Peter Jaquett, adjutant of the Delawares, fighting by his side, hastily bandaged the wound and begged him to retire. But no orders had come from Gates, now miles away in full flight. De Kalb thought the fight could still be won and he refused to retreat.
>
> The fighting was hand-to-hand. Cornwallis threw some 2000 men against the remaining 600 continental troops. De Kalb called for bayonets. De Kalb at their head, they crashed through the ranks before them, wheeled and smote them from the rear. But ball after ball had found their leader, blood poured from him, yet he found the strength to cut down another English soldier whose bayonet was at his breast. That was his last stroke. He fell, bleeding from eleven wounds.[69]

Other accounts of de Kalb's death offer yet a different story:

> During the British southern campaign, de Kalb was disappointed to learn that Horatio Gates had been appointed to command instead of him.

BARON DE KALB.

The Baron de Kalb

Baron Johann de Kalb. An engraving of the portrait by Charles Wilson Peale in the Independence Hall Museum, Philadelphia, Pennsylvania. *New York Public Library.*

Gates led the army to a disastrous defeat at Battle of Camden on August 16, 1780. De Kalb's horse was shot from under him, causing him to tumble to the ground. Before he could get up, he was shot three times and bayonetted repeatedly by British soldiers. His friend and aide, the Chevalier du Buysson, was seriously wounded blocking additional blows with his own body.

Upon seeing de Kalb Cornwallis told him, "I am sorry, sir, to see you, not sorry that you are vanquished, but sorry to see you so badly wounded." It is reported that Cornwallis supervised as de Kalb's wounds were dressed by his own surgeons. As he lay dying, de Kalb was reported to have said to a British officer, "I thank you sir for your generous sympathy, but I die the death I always prayed for: the death of a soldier fighting for the rights of man." He died three days later and was buried in Camden.[70]

Ten days after the battle, du Buysson from Charleston addressed a letter to Generals Gist and Smallwood that said (author's emphasis):

> *It is with particular pleasure I obey the baron's last command in presenting his most affectionate compliments to all the officers and men of his division.* He *expressed the greatest satisfaction in the testimony given by the British Army, of the bravery of his troops; and he was charmed with the firm opposition they made to a superior force, when abandoned by the rest of the army.* The gallant behavior of the Delaware regiment *and the companies of artillery attached to the brigades afforded him infinite pleasure.*[71]

Whichever account you believe, it is clear that Jaquett was in the thick of a very tough fight and was fortunate to escape with his life. He was surely with de Kalb in the heat of the action, which was a crushing defeat for the Delaware Regiment. Robert Kirkwood, desperately trying to keep his men engaged in the fight, waved his sword and shouted, "By the living God, the first man who falters shall receive this weapon in his craven heart!"[72] Kirkwood's words succeeded in preventing his men from running away, but roughly half of the 275 remaining soldiers became casualties. The regiment never recovered and continued on as a pair of companies fighting alongside the Marylanders.

General Nathanael Greene commented on this battle, "Though the action terminated unfavorably to the army, yet the gallant action of the light-infantry commanded by Captain Kirkwood, the cavalry under Colonel William Washington and the firmness of the Maryland troops rendered the advantage expensive to the enemy."[73]

Colonel Henry "Light-Horse Harry" Lee, a Revolutionary War hero and the father of Robert E. Lee, said, "The State of Delaware furnished one regiment only; and certainly no regiment in the army surpassed it in soldiership."[74]

The scattered remnants of the regiment assembled at Salisbury under Colonel Smallwood of the Maryland Continentals after several days on the run. The men marched on August 24 for Hillsborough as a place of rendezvous, arriving on September 6, some two hundred miles from Camden. They had been reduced to only 300 men but were soon augmented by the return of 160 recaptured American prisoners from a British formation marching to Charleston. They formed three companies of light infantry. Here they rested until October 7, awaiting clothes, arms and provisions.

General Nathanael Greene moved his Continental army to the Upper Coastal Plain's High Hills of Santee to gain relief from the heat, humidity

Left: General Nathanael Greene. *Library of Congress (LC-USZ62-16372).*

Right: General William Smallwood, Maryland Regiment. *Wikimedia Commons.*

and diseases associated with the adjacent Middle Coastal Plain swamps. On September 27, Robert Kirkwood noted in his journal that he had gone to headquarters "for Docts. Medecine for my men and returned the 30th, Inst. 40 miles."[75]

These men proved their worth once again at the Battles of Cowpens and Guilford Court House in 1781. Both Kirkwood's and Jaquett's companies operated with Henry Lee's cavalry forces, so his statement implies more than a passing familiarity with their work. On the other hand, the Delaware companies were also often used to stiffen the main battle line, such as at Cowpens and Guilford. Without dispute, we can assert that the Delaware troops were some of the most experienced veterans in the Continental army.

Cowpens (South Carolina, January 17, 1781)

The travails of the Continental army of the South were not at an end:

> *The troops were in a most shocking condition for the want of clothing, especially shoes, and we having kept open campaign all winter the troops*

LT.COL. BANASTRE TARLTON.

Above: The Battle of Cowpens, by Don Troiani. *National Guard Heritage Painting.*

Right: Lieutenant Colonel Banastre Tarleton. *New York Public Library.*

were taking sick very fast. Here the manly fortitude of the Maryland Line was very great, being obliged to march and do duty barefoot, being all the winter the chief part of them wanting coats and shoes which they bore with the greatest patience imaginable, for which their praise should never be forgotten; and indeed in all the hardships which they had undergone they never seemed to frown. [76]

A common tactic adopted by the Americans during the Southern Campaign came to be known as a "defense in depth." The practice involved forming multiple lines of battle. Each successive position engaged the attacking force and then withdrew. Such a method was designed to delay an enemy advance and inflict as many casualties as possible. Elements of Greene's army under Brigadier General Daniel Morgan utilized it against a hand-picked British force under Banastre Tarleton at the Battle of Cowpens on January 17, 1781. The engagement was a resounding American triumph. Tarleton was routed and lost 860 men of 1,100 engaged.

The Continental Flying Army of some 800 ragged, hungry troops faced Lieutenant Colonel Tarleton's force of 1,100 well-fed soldiers supported by cavalry and two cannons at Cowpens. Their forces included the Royal English Fusiliers, the First Battalion of the Seventy-First and the British Legion, horse and foot. Cowpens, South Carolina, was the scene of a classic battle, one that marked the beginning of the American campaign under General Greene to drive the British from the South.

After Tarleton's assault, the Virginians managed to outflank his forces, causing confusion. William Seymour recorded:

> *The enemy advanced and attacked our light infantry with both cannon and small arms, where meeting with a very warm reception they then thought to surround our right flank, to prevent which Captain Kirkwood with his company wheeled to the right and attacked their left flank so vigorously that they were soon repulsed, our men advancing on them so rapidly that they soon gave way.*[77]
>
> *The courage and conduct of the brave General Morgan in this action is highly commendable, as likewise Colonel Howard, who after all the time of the action rode from right to left of the line encouraging the men; and indeed all the officers and men behaved with uncommon and undaunted bravery, but more especially the brave Captain Kirkwood and his company, who that day did wonders, rushing on the enemy without either dread or fear, and being instrumental in taking a great number of prisoners.*[78]

Then the old Continentals, the veteran Delaware Blues and Marylanders, charged with bayonet and smashed the British center. The enemy fled in disorder, leaving their field pieces behind. Colonel William Washington's cavalry chased them for twenty-four miles. The Americans' loss was 12 killed and 60 wounded. The British lost 10 officers, more than 100 killed, 200 wounded and 550 taken prisoner; 100 cavalry horses, 35 wagons and 800 muskets fell into American hands. Thomas Anderson described the battle this way:

> *Before day received information that Colonel Talton [Tarleton] was within five miles of us with a strong body of horse and infantry—whereon we got up and put ourselves in order of battle—by day light they hove in sight, halted and formed the line in full view. As we had no artillery to annoy them, and the General not thinking it prudent to advance from the ground we had formed on, we looked at each other for a considerable time. About sunrise they began the attack by the discharge of two pieces of cannon and three Huzzas advancing briskly on our Riflemen that was posted in front who fought well, disputing the ground that was between them and us—flying from one tree to another; at last being forced to give ground, they fell back in our rear. The enemy seeing us standing in such*

good order halted for some time to dress their Line, which outflanked ours considerably. They then advanced on boldly, under a very heavy fire, until they got within a few yards of us, but their Line was so much longer than ours, they turned our flanks, which caused us to fall back some distance. The enemy thinking that we were broke set up a great shout, charged us with their bayonett, but in no order. We let them come within ten or fifteen yards of us, then give them a full volley, and at the same time charged them home; they not expecting any such thing, put them in such confusion that we were in amongst them with the bayonet, which caused them to give ground, and at last to take to flight; but we followed them up so close that they never could get in order again until we killed and took the whole of the Infantry prisoners. At the same time we charged, Colonel Washington charged the horse, which soon give way. We followed them ten miles, but not being able to come up with them, returned back to the field of battle that night, and lay amongst the dead and wounded, very well pleased with our day's work. Marched this day, 20 [miles].[79]

In terms of duration and actual troops engaged, it was a larger battle than Princeton; its results, the destruction of an important part of the British army in the South, were incalculable in terms of ending the war.

There followed a game of hide-and-seek as the Americans fought a war of mobility. The Delawares and Marylanders were part of a light force that included William Washington's Cavalry and Harry Lee's Light Horse. It was described as the "flower of the Southern Army." They were the rear guard, often in sight of the enemy and always on duty. They got six hours sleep for every forty-eight in a running fight through rough country.[80]

"The Delaware troops...had suffered severely at the defeat of Gates [Camden]...this little corps...was the admiration of the army and their leader, Kirkwood, was the American Diomed."[81]

CLAPP'S MILL (ALAMANCE, NORTH CAROLINA, MARCH 2, 1781)

The American light troops under Colonel Otho Holland Williams of Maryland and Lieutenant Colonel Henry "Light-Horse Harry" Lee of Virginia engaged the British light troops near Clapp's Mill on Beaver Creek. The Americans attempted to lure the British forces, under Lieutenant

Colonel Banastre Tarleton, from their camp near the mill into an ambush on Alamance Creek, where cavalry units and reinforcements lay in waiting. In heavy fighting, at least seventeen British soldiers and eight American militiamen died.

WETZELL'S MILL (NORTH CAROLINA, MARCH 6, 1781)

Cornwallis's army clashed at Adam Wetzell's Mill with advance elements of Nathanael Greene's Southern Army commanded by Colonel Otho Holland Williams. Greene dispatched Williams with the army's light infantry, mostly Maryland and Delaware Continentals, as well as several hundred Virginia riflemen led by William Preston and Hugh Crockett, to reconnoiter Cornwallis's location. Cornwallis similarly dispatched a light corps, consisting of one thousand infantry and cavalry jointly led by Lieutenant Colonel James Webster and Lieutenant Colonel Banastre Tarleton.

In the early morning hours, under the cover of a thick fog, Stuart and Tarleton advanced on Williams's position. However, alert sentries spotted the enemy movement, and Williams began a race with the British for the ford. "Light-Horse Harry" Lee's Legion and the Virginia riflemen provided covering fire for Williams, allowing his Continentals to retreat the ten miles to the ford from their starting position.

In Delaware sergeant Major William Seymour's account of the battle, he wrote:

> *On the night of the sixth, Captain Kirkwood with his company of Light Infantry and about forty riflemen was detached off in order to surprise Colonel Tarleton who lay encamped on the other side of the Allamance; which having approached at about one o'clock in the morning and going himself with a guide to reconnoiter their lines, where finding which way their pickets were posted, upon which he ordered the whole to move on, having formed a line of battle. When we came upon the sentinels, they challenged very briskly, and no answer being made, upon which they immediately discharged their pieces and ran in to their guard. We took one of the sentinels off his post at the same time and obliged him to show us where the guard lay, upon which we fired very briskly on them. By this time the camp was all alarmed, Colonel Tarleton retreating in great confusion towards the main army, commanded by Lord Cornwallis, about two miles*

from this place; when meeting a party of Tories and mistaking them for our militia, he charged on them very furiously, putting great numbers to the sword. On the other hand, they taking Colonel Tarleton for our horses and infantry there commenced a smart skirmish, in which great numbers of the Tories were sent to the lower regions.[82]

Having crossed the ford, Williams decided to make a defensive stand. The Continentals provided the main line of defense, while the Virginia riflemen and dragoons from Lee's Legion and the Third Continental Light Dragoons protected the flanks. The first British assault across the creek failed, but a second, personally led by Lieutenant Colonel Webster, forced the Americans to retreat. The fighting left thirty British soldiers lying wounded or killed. Lee's Legion lost two killed and three wounded, while eight Virginians died and seventeen were wounded.

GUILFORD COURT HOUSE (NORTH CAROLINA, MARCH 15, 1781)

The armies met once again at Guilford Court House, North Carolina. It was the site of the culminating battle in General Greene's campaign against General Cornwallis. The Flying Army sustained and repulsed a charge.

Greene employed the defense in depth method again against Cornwallis's main army at Guilford Court House on March 15. At this point, the Delawares were separated into two companies. Captain Peter Jacquett led the first company within the First Maryland Regiment, while Captain Robert Kirkwood led the second as a light infantry company. A second heavy attack was withstood when the British regulars fell back across a ravine. Although Greene lost the battle, Cornwallis's forces were so depleted that he retreated to the coast and from there moved to Virginia, where he was ultimately to meet his fate at Yorktown.

The First Maryland Regiment and Steen's Virginia militia bore the pain, but Kirkwood's light infantry all gave proof of a high degree of valor and steadfastness. "Except the infantry of the Legion, and Kirkwood's little corps of Delawares," says William Johnson in his *Life of Greene*, published in 1822, "the First Regiment of Maryland was the only body of men in the American Army who could be compared to the enemy in discipline and experience." Kirkwood's company lost three killed and six wounded.

Above: Battle of Guilford Court House, March 15, 1781, by Charles McBarron Jr. *Wikimedia Commons.*

Left: Lord Cornwallis. *Library of Congress (LC-USZ62-45340).*

Victory did not solve Cornwallis's key problems. Greene's army remained intact and the country hostile. Although Cornwallis drove Greene from the field, the engagement cost him 25 percent of his command. Cornwallis's army had sustained heavy casualties and was exhausted and short of supplies. Sickness, wounds, desertion and losses at Guilford had reduced it to about 1,500 effectives. He decided to retreat southeast to Wilmington on the coast to get reinforcements and supplies. He arrived there in early April. Meanwhile, Greene moved behind him into South Carolina to attack Lord Rawdon's force at Camden.

Between April 1780 and April 1781, the Delawares had marched above 2,600 miles, besides being engaged in many skirmishes and two pitched battles. They had passed through or over a score of streams that would have been reckoned large rivers in any other country in the world. Shoeless and in rags, and laden with their heavy firelocks, they plodded through the wilderness for month after month of a never-ending campaign without showing any perceptible diminution in their martial ardor. After a lost battle, which was a familiar experience for them, they almost instantaneously recovered their self-confidence and their self-complacency, with the invaluable elasticity of the American soldier.[83]

Logtown (South Carolina, April 19, 1781)

On the nineteenth, Greene's army marched to "Sands Hills" (Hobkirk's Hill), within two miles of Camden, where he camped. By evening, his light troops then skirmished with some of Lord Rawdon's forces, including some of the New York Volunteers and the Volunteers of Ireland, outside the Camden fortifications (i.e., Logtown) for the next few days. Kirkwood's journal records:

19 [April] *Marched within 4 miles of Camden, took Eleven of the Enemy prisoners…15* [miles] *This evening Genl. Green gave me orders if possible to take possession of Logtown, which was in full view of Camden & if I could take it, to mentain it until further orders, Leaving Camp about 8 at night, arrived before the town between 9 & 10 and about 12 Oclock got full possession of the place, A scattered firing was kept up all night, And at sun rise next morning, had a sharp schirmage, Beat in the Enemy, About two hours afterwards had the Very agreeable Sight of the advance of the Army. 20th. This day Col. Washington with my Infantry went Westerly round*

Camden, Burnt a house in one of the Enemys Redoubts on the Wateree River;
took 40 horses and fifty Head of cattle and returned to Camp…4 [miles].[84]

At 10:00 p.m. on April 19, Captain Robert Kirkwood and his Delaware Continentals advanced toward Camden under the cover of darkness. By midnight, he had full possession of Logtown, but the firing continued all night. At sunrise on the twentieth, there was a sizeable skirmish again, but Captain Kirkwood beat in the pickets. From his position, he was able to see the advance works of the British army in Camden. The next day, Major General Greene arrived near Logtown, a half mile from the British works in Camden, and set up his camp.

On April 21, Captain Kirkwood and Lieutenant Colonel William Washington conducted a diversionary raid into Camden. They burned one house, captured forty horses and captured fifty head of cattle on a foraging expedition.

Hobkirk's Hill (South Carolina, April 25, 1781)

The Battle of Hobkirk's Hill (sometimes referred to as the Second Battle of Camden) was a battle fought near Camden, South Carolina. A young prisoner of war, future president Andrew Jackson witnessed the battle from his prison cell. A force under Nathanael Greene defended a ridge known as Hobkirk's Hill against an attack by an even smaller British force led by Francis Rawdon. After a fierce clash, Greene retreated a few miles,

The Battle of Hobkirk's Hill. Charge of Colonel Washington's cavalry against the British right flank to cover the American retreat, by F.C. Yohn. *New York Public Library*.

leaving Rawdon's soldiers in possession of the hill.[85] Captain Kirkwood and the Delaware Regiment gallantly received and returned the fire of the British van and kept them at bay while Greene formed his army.[86] Kirkwood's losses were five wounded and three captured, including two of the wounded.

On May 4, Kirkwood noted in his journal, "March'd to the Ferry and took the Redoubt, and burned the Block House on the South side of the Wateree, the Return'd to the Army at the 25 Mile Creek."[87]

Kirkwood's light infantry was assigned as a corps of observation at Sandy's. Kirkwood noted on May 8, 1781, "The enemy was within two miles of us before we knew of them being out when our Vadet [vidette—a mounted sentinel stationed in advance of pickets] Came in and inform'd. We then Drew up an order of battle and lay in their Sight of [each] other until Evening," when the enemy retired and the corps of observation marched up to rejoin the army.[88]

Kirkwood wrote on May 21:

> *Was ordered with Col. Washington's Horse to Surprise a party of tories under command of Col. Young; Coming up to a place found it evacuated, the Horse let me, with expectation to Come up with them while I moved on at Leisure. The Tories taking us for some of themselves come out of a Swamp in our Rear, & being undeceived took one of my men prisoner; upon which A Firing Commenced, but they being on horseback pushed off with the loss of one man Killed & one Horse taken, A Short time Afterwards the Horse joined me, and before Dark killed four more taking six prisoners: Marched this day 23 miles.[89]*

NINETY SIX (SOUTH CAROLINA, MAY 22, 1781)

Greene's army came upon a Tory stockade camp called Ninety Six held by 550 men. The American force was down to 100 and the Delawares to only 60 remaining soldiers. Some Loyalists came out of the swamps and woods and mistook Captain Kirkwood as their own kind, since they were in hunting frocks and had not fired upon them. They eventually recognized the Delaware Continentals as their enemy and took one of them as prisoner, firing on the rest. Captain Kirkwood returned fire and killed one man. The rest of the Loyalists took off. On June 18, they took the main stockade. There followed three months of marching advances and retreats. In four weeks, Kirkwood's little band marched 360 miles, crossing ten rivers. Their food had been miserably scanty. Kirkwood recorded, "Rice furnished our substitute for bread....Of meat we had literally none....Frogs abounded...and on them chiefly did the light troops subsist. Even the alligator was used by a few."[90]

During the largely desultory war in the South, Kirkwood's crack company of light troops operated regularly as infantry support for dragoons under the command of Colonels William Washington and Henry Lee. Kirkwood's services were clearly highly valued by both officers, and Lee in particular formed a close working relationship with the Delaware captain. On June 29, 1781, Kirkwood, who was then attached to Lee's troops, received orders from Washington to join his command. Lee countermanded the order, explaining to General Greene that it was necessary "least an opportunity of striking might be lost...for want of force." Hoping to forestall any squabbling, Lee asked Greene to notify Washington "least a stupid jealousy may arise."[91]

EUTAW SPRINGS (SOUTH CAROLINA, SEPTEMBER 8, 1781)

At Eutaw Springs, Greene attacked an equal force of British regulars. This was, by far, the bloodiest battle of Greene's campaign. Two Maryland battalions under Lieutenant Colonel John Eager Howard and Major Henry Hardman, as well as Lieutenant Colonel William Washington's mounted men and Captain Robert Kirkwood's Delaware infantry companies, formed the tail of the American column. According to Kirkwood, his men were in the "Corps de Reserve" during the battle, positioned behind a front line of militia from the Carolinas and a second line "with North Carolinah regulars, Virginians and Marylanders." He reported that "we arrived within [a] mile of [the British] Encampment, where we met their front line which soon brought the action general, we Drove their first and Second Lines, took upwards of 500 prisoners...[but] our men were so spent for want of water, and Our Continental Officers suffering much in the Action, rendered it advisable for Gen. Green to Draw off his Army."

The fighting was hot and fierce. A bayonet charge, which was becoming a Delaware specialty, broke the British line, recapturing a cannon from the Redcoats, which they rolled back to rebel lines. William Washington's

The Battle of Eutaw Springs, from the Emmet Collection of Manuscripts. *New York Public Library.*

cavalry were caught in a cross-fire, and half of them fell. The Delaware Blues hurried to the rescue of their old friends and drove the British back. The battle was indecisive, and the Americans withdrew. Kirkwood's men and a party of Virginians were the last to leave the field. His journal says, "Found our army had withdrawn from the field, made it necessary for us to likewise withdraw. Brought off one of the enemy's three pounders through a thick woods for near four miles, without the assistance of but one horse."[92]

Despite winning a tactical victory, the British lost strategically. Their inability to stop Greene's continuing operations forced them to abandon most of their conquests in the South, leaving them in control of a small number of isolated enclaves at Wilmington, Charleston and Savannah. General Greene, in his report to Congress, said, "I think myself primarily indebted for the victory to the free use of the bayonet made by the Virginia and Maryland brigades and to the Delaware troops for their unparalleled bravery and heroism."[93]

In this encounter, the Marylanders and Kirkwood's Delaware Blues held the army together once again and achieved Greene's strategic objectives.[94] The British attempt to pacify the South with Loyalist support had failed even before Cornwallis surrendered at Yorktown:

At Eutaw Springs, many of the Continental infantry, the cloth of whose coats had long rotted off them in fragments "fought with pieces of moss tied on the shoulder and flank to keep the musket and cartridge box from galling." They sometimes got nothing for ten or twelve days running except half a pound of flour and a morsel of beef, "so miserably poor that scarce any mortal could make use of it," and were fain to live upon green corn, and unripe apples and peaches. During the pursuit of Cornwallis after Guilford Court House, many of them fainted on the road for lack of food.[95]

Cornwallis now faced a major decision. Should he return to South Carolina to help Rawdon or go elsewhere? He wrote to Clinton on April 10 that he thought it best to move north into Virginia and link up with a British army corps there. He argued that he was too far away to reach Rawdon in time and that the Carolinas could be subdued only when Virginia was securely under British control. But he gave another major reason for his preference: only by moving north could he "hope to preserve the troops, from the fatal sickness, which so nearly ruined the army last autumn."[96]

Surrender of Cornwallis at Yorktown. *Library of Congress (LC-USZ62-39587).*

In September 1781, British general Cornwallis retreated to Yorktown, where Washington and his French allies besieged the British forces. Delaware troops were present here as well, although not Kirkwood's companies.

In August 1781, a contingent of Delaware soldiers under Captains William McKennan and Paul Quenoualt was assigned to General Henry Knox's artillery corps. In that capacity, they contributed to the victory at Yorktown. To many, the surrender at Yorktown in the fall of 1781 brought the Revolutionary War to an end, but it was not quite over. Delaware's Kirkwood simply noted in his journal from South Carolina, "Received Intelligence of the Surrender of Lord Cornwallace's whole Army to his Excelency Genl. George Washington in York Town Virginia." On November 22, 1781, "This day was ordered to march by the way of Howell's Ferry to Col Thompson's and there to join the Army. The troops moved, but I went to Capt Howells having the ague & Fever where I stayed untill the 27th Inst."[97]

The Delaware men then marched south to join General Nathanael Greene's forces on January 4, 1782, completing a trek of 550 miles. Here they were united with Jaquett and Kirkwood. This enabled several officers from the Delaware regiment—including Kirkwood and Jaquett—to return home on furlough after six years of fighting, affording relief to a small group of soldiers who had "long and faithfully and with conspicuous gallantry" served the cause of American independence.[98]

The Journey Home

Both Kirkwood and Jaquett left accounts of their respective homeward journeys. Kirkwood, in his usual brief style, noted in his journal the stages from headquarters to his home in Newark, Delaware. On January 1, 1782, Kirkwood, who had only briefly seen his home in six years, was granted a furlough. He started on January 4, 1782, without the other officers, who had been relieved by the arrival of McKennan's recruits. He made no notes until March 4, arriving at Hillsborough and rendezvousing with Captain Jaquett, Lieutenants Anderson and Campbell, Ensign Platt and Dr. Hartley of South Carolina, who accompanied him.

On the thirteenth, Kirkwood crossed the Roanoke and "[s]topped at Mr. Deloanes's who is termed a Col. In that County, & no doubt thinks himself a Gentleman, but shall leave the readers to Judge, whether or not, When they are informed by this that after General Sinclier [St. Clair] had remained at his House one night, the next morning had to pay three guineas, after having been invited there. In a few weeks afterwards Col. O.H. Williams called at the same house, but could not get quarters....I, not knowing his Character, shared the same fate...indeed he turned my wagon off Plantation....I requested only the floor to lay on which was refused me & rather than Quarrel with one of the first rank in the famous State of Virginia, chose to Lay in the Woods."[99]

At Petersburg, Kirkwood and Jaquett parted ways on March 17. Jaquett, Hartly and the wagon "went round by land." While Kirkwood, Campbell, Anderson and Platt "went on Board a Vessel at the Broad Way Bound to the Head of Elk." The next day, their boat was taken by a small vessel from New York called *Hook-in Sneevy*, but Kirkwood's party escaped in a small boat. At Nottingham Court House, they boarded another, bound for Head of Elk.

On April 1, they set out on foot "for Yocommico river, Crossed over the Potowmick" and by the fourth were in Annapolis. There they embarked again for Head of Elk on the seventh, "arrived at Newark about eight O'Clock in the Evening." "Total of marches From the 13th of April 1780 [when he left Morristown]...5006 miles."

By the following year, the Delaware troops still under Kirkwood's command had followed him north—one detachment stationed in Philadelphia and the other in Newark, Delaware.

From Philadelphia, Kirkwood wrote to the commander-in-chief and requested that the troops be consolidated at New Castle, Delaware, where he could better attend to the lax "Morals of the Men," which had been compromised due to the seedy influences of Philadelphia. A transfer to New Castle, thought Kirkwood, "may have a powerful tendency, in checking their horrid ravages." The tough campaigning of the previous two years had kept Kirkwood too busy to properly enforce regulations, or as he put it, "The severity of the southern Campaigns has prevented that Regularity, and Discipline so necessary."[100] With major campaigning all but over, little was needed from the Delaware troops but idle garrison duty. Washington decided, for the time being, to leave the Delaware detachments where they were.

At the end of the war, when Lord Cornwallis surrendered at Yorktown, General Greene placed Jaquett in charge of a party of sick and wounded men, with instructions to convey them home, which he succeeded in doing despite many hardships.

Jaquett described his journey in a petition addressed to the General Assembly:

Gen. Greene, well knowing the privations, fatigue, and hardships that Captain Kirkwood & myself had passed through during our Southern Campaigns politely offered to send us home on command with orders to the Comesary & Quartermasters Department to furnish us with provisions & forage at every Depot on the road. Capt. Kirkwood left Headquarters two days before me with a view of taking his route as much as possible by water and I began my march on the 20 Day February, with four officers, nine invalid Soldiers, one woman, two wagons and nine Horses, but unfortunately your memmorlist found neither provisions or forage in any of the public stores.

It is known that the army had not received one cent of pay during all our Southern Campaigns, that Continental money had depreciated 100 for one—and we had a march of more than 500 miles, without our pay, rations, forage or one dollar of the public money, and we could not obtain one single article of provision or forage on the whole route without the hard cash layed down, thus situated I paid from my own private resources $168.45 as per account rendered of which I have never received one cent. At that time the United States was indebted to me Upwards of 3000 Dols. Exclusive of the sd. Amount for pay, commutation of half pay, Depreciation of pay &c. which was afterwards payed by giving a certificate which our wants obliged us to sell at a discount of 66 pr. Sent—and his [Jaquett's] patrimonial Estate was but very small & that small sum much reduced in the Revolutionary War, it may be asked where he got $168.45 cents, he answers that a Noble Harted Lady, a friend of the revolution of respectable family and fortune furnished him all that money in "English Guineas," at a time when he had scarcely a Shirt on his back, or a means of getting one, or a shoe on his feet, without asking a scratch of the pen for its return, that Lady has long since descended to the tomb, but your memmorlist still holds himself honor bound to make retribution to her heirs—Your Memmorlist therefore respectfully asks your Honorable boddy to give him the above sum with interest from the 20 of February 1782 and although he is too old to fight, he will Pray.[101]

In later years, he repaid the full amount to her heirs, with principle and interest amounting to more than $500. Jaquett and his band of invalids arrived home at last on January 17, 1783, after marching 720 miles from Petersburg, Virginia. They were mustered out of service at Christiana Bridge on November 3, 1783.[102]

Kirkwood and Jaquett's accounts differ on the dates of departure from South Carolina. Kirkwood's account was set down at the time, while Jaquett's was written many years later.

The war left most officers' personal finances badly neglected. Kirkwood and the remaining officers of the Delaware regiment unanimously agreed to forego the half-pay for life that was their due as veteran officers, requesting instead "commutation," or a lump-sum payment of five years' full pay.[103] In practice, most officers requesting commutation received not cash but nearly worthless "commutation certificates." Kirkwood's impressive combat record would initially earn him little more than hollow honorifics from the cash-strapped young republic.

The Delaware Continental Regiment had remained in service for more than seven years, seeing action in every major campaign of the Revolution but one. Its fifteen official battle honors read like a history of the war: Long Island, New York, 1776–77; Trenton; Princeton; Brandywine; Germantown; Monmouth; Camden; Cowpens; Guilford Court House; and Yorktown. After the Battle of Camden, the regiment was so reduced in numbers it had to be reorganized as two companies under command of two captains, the gallant Robert Kirkwood and the brave Peter Jaquett.

Kirkwood recorded in his journal a cumulative total of 5,006 miles traveled just between April 1780 and April 1782 during the Southern Campaign. A cursory read of this journal reveals an astounding procession of marches. No other regiment served in more campaigns than the First Delaware Regiment. Kirkwood had served from beginning to end with the Delaware Regiment. Only Captain Peter Jaquett equaled Kirkwood in service without capture or death during the Southern Campaign. He had served for seven years and ten months in thirty-two battles and skirmishes.[104]

The lessons we learn are that Delawareans responded to the cause of freedom not only near home but also far away. They fought bravely while facing great odds and persevered to win back the ground they lost. At the end of the war, the remaining 120 Delaware Continentals marched seven hundred miles home from South Carolina—33 of them having served and survived the entire war.

The Delaware Continentals enlisted for the duration of the war and were promised a bounty of twenty dollars and one hundred acres of land to them or their survivors postbellum. During the course of the war, Delaware enlisted more than four thousand men, but at its close, this was reduced to just two companies, as they had been decimated by battle and death. Delawareans are rare on the pension lists, as few survived to partake of their reward. To their native state's everlasting shame, few of those who survived were given their just reward.

Chapter 6

POSTWAR

Kirkwood After the War (1784–91)

At the close of the war, September 30, 1783, Kirkwood was brevetted to the rank of major and returned to Newark, Delaware. In recognition of his service during the Revolution, Delaware gave Robert Kirkwood one hundred pounds (Delaware was then using British units for currency). He married Sarah England. They had a son, Joseph R., in 1784 and a daughter, Mary, as well as an infant who died. The couple pursued a "mercantile business." They moved to Odessa and then to St. Georges Station (now called Kirkwood), where Sarah died in 1787. After Sarah's death, Kirkwood left his children in the care of relatives and headed west.

Also in 1787, Robert Kirkwood paid $2,204 to buy 260 acres of land in Jefferson County of the Northwest Territory (previously Virginia, now Ohio). Kirkwood built a stout log cabin. It became known as Kirkwood's Blockhouse. It was constructed as a stronghold against possible (and likely) Indian incursions on the then frontier. Settlers at that time were isolated and sparse. He was a justice of the peace in that area in 1790. Kirkwood was one of the founders of what is now the town of Bridgeport, Ohio, six miles northwest of what is now Wheeling, West Virginia. In 1788, the State of Virginia gave Robert Kirkwood 1,920 acres of land in Belmont County in the Northwest Territory (twenty miles south of his land in Jefferson Company).

Jean Lattré, *Carte des Etats-Unis de l'Amerique suivant le Traité de Paix de 1783*. The United States and Great Britain exchanged documents confirming their ratification of the Treaty of Paris in May 1784. The next month, Jean Lattré, an official engraver to Louis XVI, published this large-scale map—the first map to delineate the full extent of the new United States of America after the ratification of the treaty. The elaborate cartouche depicts a sailor hanging medallions bearing the Great Seal of the United States, the insignia of the Society of the Cincinnati and the arms of Benjamin Franklin (to whom the map is dedicated) on the highest yard aboard the new ship of state. *American Revolution Institute of the Society of the Cincinnati.*

The Northwest Territory had been ceded by the British to the Americans as part of the settlement of the Revolutionary War, but the British encouraged the Indians who inhabited the area to fight the new settlers. The Indians were a confederation of the Shawnee, Delaware, Ottowa, Iroquois, Chippewa, Miami and Pottawatomi tribes. Indian war parties continued to strike settlements from Pennsylvania to Kentucky, as well as settlers' convoys headed downstream on the Ohio River. Militia raids into the tribal heartland, as well as a humiliating defeat of federal forces in the autumn of 1790, failed to stem the flow of Indian attacks.

In March 1791, an expedition under the command of the governor of the Northwest Territory, Arthur St. Clair, set out to build a line of forts. Robert Kirkwood was commissioned a captain in the Second Regiment of U.S. Infantry (one company of which was raised in Delaware). St. Clair's army was to rendezvous at Cincinnati before striking north toward the Miami heartland at the headwaters of the Maumee River. Over the succeeding months, recruits began making their way down the Ohio River.[105]

During the middle of April, Indian attacks increased in the vicinity of Wheeling, and on May 2, one of the war parties struck Kirkwood's home. Fortunately, the captain wasn't alone. A detachment of soldiers was present when the cabin came under attack, and after a spirited fight, the Indians were driven off. Eastern newspapers reported, "A body of about 40 Indians attacked the house of Robert Kirkwood, opposite the mouth of the Wheeling, killed a Sergeant Walker…and wounded Ensign Biggs and three of his men."[106]

When St. Clair finally pushed north from Cincinnati in September 1791, he was woefully behind schedule, badly supplied and at the head of an undisciplined mob of raw recruits. Kirkwood, who had commanded some of the finest infantry in the Continental army, led far different makings into the wilderness. Adjutant General Winthrop Sargent would write that most of the troops had been recruited "from the offscourings of large towns and cities" and were utterly incompetent in "the arduous duties of Indian warfare." Even Kirkwood's Second Regiment, thought Sargent, was hastily "brought into the field, without time for instruction and never having fired even a blank cartridge."[107] It was a recipe for disaster.

For his part, Robert Kirkwood seems to have been sick for much of the campaign. Writing from the newly constructed Fort Hamilton on October 3, Captain Samuel Newman wrote, "I am ye. only Capt. in our regt. Who is well enof to do duty. Kirkwood has been confin'd ever since we came here."[108] The following day, the army forded the Great Miami River in frigid water up to their waists. Although a number of convalescents were left behind, Kirkwood accompanied his men. According to Captain Jacob Slough, Kirkwood was something of a living legend in the officer corps; men who had heard of his exploits during the Revolution would "speak of him in the most exalted terms." Kirkwood took Slough under his wing, the latter writing that "we became fast friends." "I passed many nights with him on guard," wrote Slough, "and benefitted greatly from his experience." Apparently, Kirkwood remained ill as the army groped its way north over the following month. Slough recalled that Kirkwood had been sick during the first few days of November but "was always ready for duty."[109]

BATTLE OF MIAMI (OHIO, NOVEMBER 4, 1781)

On the morning of November 4, 1791, about one thousand Natives of the Indian confederacy struck St. Clair's encampment at the headwaters of the Wabash River. In a furious fight that lasted a harrowing three hours, the American army was cut to pieces in what would prove to be the worst American defeat of the nation's Indian Wars. At the outset of the fighting, Slough caught sight of Kirkwood "cheering his men," but at some point the Delaware captain was badly wounded and helped to the rear. When Slough was shot through his right arm and went to have the wound dressed, he found his "friend Kirkwood lying against the root of a tree, shot through the abdomen, and in great pain."[110]

Slough returned to his own company, but when the American position began to collapse, he ran to Kirkwood and "proposed having him carried off." Painfully gripping what was clearly a mortal wound in his stomach, Kirkwood brushed him off. "No, I am dying," Kirkwood said, "save yourself if you can, and leave me to my fate." According to Slough's account, the dying Kirkwood then uttered the unthinkable and asked Slough to shoot him. The Indians were closing in fast, and Kirkwood is reputed to have said, "God knows how they will treat me." For Slough, it was a nightmarish ordeal. "You can better judge of my feelings than I can describe them," he would later write. "I shook him by the hand, and left him to his fate."[111]

In a desperate attempt to save the remnants of his army, St. Clair was forced to leave his wounded on the field. Obviously revealing a good bit of angst over the decision to abandon the wounded, Major Ebenezer Denny later explained that there was no alternative. "Delay was death," he recorded in his diary, "no preparation could be made; numbers of brave men must be left a sacrifice."[112] Among those left to their fate on the battlefield was Robert Kirkwood. Although the particulars of his final terrifying moments will never be known, it was no doubt a horrific end. A handful of survivors were taken captive, but victorious tribesmen scalped, mutilated and dismembered nearly all of the abandoned American casualties. In all, the army reported a loss of 630 killed and 283 wounded.[113]

On February 1, 1792, a burial detail returned to the site of the disaster. Winthrop Sargent described a grisly spectacle that he would never forget. The corpses of the fallen were "mangled and butchered with the most savage barbarity; and indeed, there seems to have been no act of indecent cruelty or torture which was not practiced on this occasion, to the women as well as men." The burial detail was unable to complete the job, explained Sargent, as the bodies were frozen to the ground and were "breaking to pieces in tearing them up."[114] Another army burial party arrived at the site on Christmas Day 1793. George Will recalled that "when we went to lay down in our tents at night, we had to scrape the bones together and carry them out, to make our beds."[115] Will thought that the burial party interred about six hundred jumbled sets of bones. The final resting place of Robert Kirkwood remains unknown; if indeed the indomitable soldier's remains were ever recovered, they were, appropriately, buried alongside those of his men.[116]

Henry Leethou said of Kirkwood:

> *The remnant of that corps* [the Delaware Regiment]...*from the Battle of Camden, was commanded by Captain Kirkwood, who passed through the war with high reputation; and yet, as the line of Delaware consisted but of one regiment and that regiment was reduced to a captain's command, Kirkwood could never be promoted to regular routine....The sequel is singularly hard. Kirkwood retired upon peace, a captain; and when the army under St. Claire was raised to defend the West from the Indian enemy, this veteran resumed his sword as the eldest captain in the oldest regiment.*
>
> *In the decisive defeat of the 4th November* [1791, the Battle of Miami] *the gallant Kirkwood fell, bravely sustaining his point in the action. It was the thirty-third time he had risked his life for his country; and he died as he had lived, the brave meritorious, unrewarded Kirkwood.*[117]

LEGACY

Virginia had recognized his services by a grant of two thousand acres of land in the Northwest Territory, now the state of Ohio, to which place he removed after the war. His own state never rewarded him.

Of Kirkwood's children and grandchildren, Joseph Kirkwood, Sarah and Robert Kirkwood's only son, was brought up in Delaware and married Margaret Emily Gillespie there. He moved to Belmont, Ohio, in 1806. There they had eight daughters and a son. The son died as an infant. Joseph and Margaret Kirkwood died and were buried in Bridgeport, Ohio.

Mary Kirkwood, Sarah and Robert Kirkwood's only daughter, married first a Mr. Boyer and second Arthur Whiteley (also his second marriage) of Dorchester County, Maryland. The Whiteleys had only one child, Robert Henry Kirkwood Whiteley, who served as an officer in the Quartermaster Corps of the U.S. Army during the Civil War and was promoted to brigadier general in 1865. In 1896, he died in Baltimore, Maryland, and was buried with his parents at the cemetery of the Head of Christiana Presbyterian Church.

The most fitting eulogies for Kirkwood came from the comrades who served with him. Every soldier who left a written record of the fallen captain spoke of him with the highest regard. Hezekiah Ford thought "Captain Kirkwood certainly was an officer of much respectability and distinction." Guilford Dudley described him as "a brave and experienced officer, who had fought in every considerable battle…with great and unsullied reputation."[118] William Seymour described Kirkwood as an officer "whose heroick valour and undaunted bravery must needs be recorded in history till after ages."[119] An authority no less than Nathanael Greene thought that "[n]o Man deserves better of his Country than Capt Kirkwood."[120]

MONUMENTS

An obelisk monument now marks the battle area in Ohio. The area that Robert Kirkwood settled in Belmont County is named Kirkwood Township. The town of Kirkwood, Ohio, in Shelby County (five miles south of Sidney off Route 75) may be named after a different Kirkwood family who settled there.

Delaware belatedly recognized Robert Kirkwood's life and death in service to his nation by naming a town and a highway after him. Kirkwood, Delaware, is located eight miles southeast of Newark, and the Robert Kirkwood Highway (Route 2) connects Newark to Wilmington and passes close by Polly Drummond Hill, where he was born.

JAQUETT AFTER THE WAR

Returning home to Wilmington, Peter Jaquett was in broken health, and his estate was in ruin from his absence. The dikes alongside the river had been breached, and his farmlands flooded while he was gone. He had the responsibility for an aged mother and an infirm sister. His physician recommended a voyage to the West Indies in search of renewed vigor, but he had no money to spend on such a trip. Joseph Tatnall, a Wilmington miller, offered to donate 1,200 pounds of flour to finance the trip, which covered Jaquett's expenses. He returned in good health and repaid the debt before his passing.[121]

Above: *St. Clair's Defeat*. This painting, by Rufus Fairchild Zogbaum, accompanied Theodore Roosevelt's article on St. Clair's defeat, as featured in the February 1896 issue of *Harper's New Monthly Magazine*. *Wikimedia Commons*.

Left: George Read, 1733–1798. *Library of Congress (LC-USZ62-6155)*.

Few can claim a record of service as long and distinguished as Peter Jaquett, among the first to enlist and the last to muster out of military service during the Revolution. When he attempted to vote during the fall election, he was astonished to learn that he was denied the vote by legislator George Read, who had spent the war comfortably at home.[122] Jaquett's out-of-state service meant that they "had become Aliens and that in law and justice, we had not a right to Vote." Jaquett wondered if "I should again be obliged to force a right for which I had contended for more than seven years in the field." Jaquett claimed that Read had "persecuted every man that was active in securing the independence of this country" because they had "wrestled it away from the power of his much-loved king." It should be noted that Read had voted against independence, forcing Caesar Rodney's ride to break the deadlock vote from Delaware. Federalist Read was in the forefront in repealing the anti-Loyalist Act in the state legislature after the war.

The election day crowd grew angry, and Read grew "anxious for the personal safety of himself and friends." Read at last permitted the soldiers to vote.[123]

Jaquett had other difficulties upon his return to civilian life. He applied for positions during the presidencies of both Washington and later Jefferson, but despite being a Revolutionary War hero, he never received a political appointment from either (which, being a staunch Republican, he blamed on political partisanship). He complained bitterly that the Tories against whom he had fought now were all office holders, while Revolutionary War veterans like himself were poorly recognized for their efforts.

A number of Delaware citizens recommended Jaquett to George Washington. On March 12, 1789, James Tilton wrote that Jaquett's "small patrimonial estate has been rendered unproductive, by the overflowing tide through breaches in the Wilmington banks…that five years interest on his depreciation debt is the only substantial benefit he has ever received from his public securities, and so unfriendly to the army creditors is the Government of Delaware, as to afford no regular prospect of further relief until the general government shall be able to interpose, with more than recommendatory powers." On April 13, David Finney and John Thompson, both judges of the Delaware Supreme Court, assured Washington that Jaquett's appointment "would give great Pleasure to the Virtuous Citizens" of New Castle County. A letter signed by members of the Delaware legislature testified that Jaquett's "distinguished services in the Army, have greatly endeared him to his Countrymen, and particularly to his brother officers and soldiers. Some inevitable misfortunes that have happened to his patrimonial estate, and the present low state of public credit, have reduced him to the necessity of making application for some post of profit under your Excellency's direction." In his letter to Washington, Jaquett also enclosed a supporting letter from John Dickinson to Richard Bassett from March 24, 1789.

Jaquett's letter to General Washington read:

Wilmington [Del.] *18th April 1789*

Sir,

A series of misfortune since the conclusion of the late War oblidges me to trouble your Excellency with this application—After having served to the end of the War, I returned to my farm in expectation of a convenient subsistance at least, but the winds and the waters have conspired to overwhelm my little Plantation, and the unrightious Government of Delaware has deprived me of the only fund, by which I could have fortified against these furious Elements. In short sir, the small parcel of Land which I hold, consists chiefly of the low grounds and meadows near Wilmington, which by the breaking of the Banks, have been constantly overflowed for several years, and I have not the means of repairing the Banks and reclaiming the marshes; those aids, which might have been expected from our publick securities, we have been deprived of, by the prevailing Politic's of this State.

This short history may serve to inform Your Excellency, that I am in a situation not very easy or happy, and will Appologize I hope for troubling you with an Application for some Appointment under the new Government.

I confess to your Excellency, that the Naval Office and Collectorship of Wilmington, would be most agreeable to me, But, if I should not be so happy as to obtain either of them, a militery appointment would oblidge me much, And I flatter myself Sir, that there is yet in your Excellencys Breast, an Advocate in favour of those Officers of your Army who served through a Doubtfull War as good soldiers, and have lived since the Peace as honest and peaceable Citizens, And as I am the only Officer who has served in the Line of the Delaware State that will make application to your Excellency at present, I flatter myself with success.

When I recollect how accurately your Excellency used to recognize and discriminate each and every officer of your Army, I cannot but flatter myself that I am not entirely unknown as a soldier, notwithstanding the three last years of my service I was detached from your Excellency, under the more immediate Command of that verry excellent and respectable Officer Major General Green. I shall rely upon these recommendations to obtain

Your Excellency's favour and Patronage, rather than on the influence of the great. I have the Honour to be with the greatest Affection, Your Excellencys, most Obt Humb. servt

Peter Jaquett

A letter from George Washington to Alexander Hamilton sheds some light on the rejection:

[Head of Elk, Maryland, September 16, 1791]

Dr. Sir,
Whilst I was in Wilmington waiting breakfast to day, I made the best enquiry time & circumstances would permit, for some fit character to fill the office lately held by Doctr. Latimer. Several persons were mentioned, but the weight of information was in favor of one Andrew Barratt. He was spoken of by Mr. Vining as a man of respectable character, of decision and temper. He now is, or lately has been high Sheriff of the county of Kent; & no man, it is said, could have discharged the duties of that Office better. Mr. Bedford, though he had another person in view, (Majr. Jacquet), accords in this opinion of Barratt. Doctor Latimer, whom I afterwards called upon, at New port, for the purpose of enquiry, also speaks well of Barratt. He did indeed, before I mentioned the name of Barratt to him, say that he thought Majr. Patten of Dover the best person that readily occurred to him for this office, but yielded a ready assent to the qualifications of Barratt. None knows whether he would, or would not accept the appointment. Among other things, urged in his favor by Mr. Vining, are his living near the centre of the State—amidst the Stills, and where the most discontent is said to be. To Mr. Chew of Philada. Mr. Vining particularly appeals for the character of Mr. Barratt.
If his testimony is in favor of this character, I think it will be an eligible appointment. A blank commission, signed, has been left with Mr. Lear for the Supervisor of the Delaware District.

With much esteem & regard I am Dear Sir, Your Mo: Obt. Servant

G: Washington
Head of Elk
16th. Septr. 1791.[124]

Marriage

On February 26, 1794, Peter Jaquett at age thirty-nine married Elizabeth Price (November 25, 1769–May 5, 1834), age twenty-four, of Chester, Pennsylvania, the daughter of Elisha Price. She served as a "Member of Provincial Committee." Their otherwise happy marriage would be childless, which may account for his fondness for children. They settled down to a tranquil life of pastoral pleasures.

Yet the restless Jaquett pursued the war pension he was promised in the form of land until his final years. It is unclear if he was ever successful. The Bounty-Warrant papers from the Library of Virginia contain correspondence between Jaquett and the governor of Virginia (he had fought in Virginia), who had sole power to grant these kinds of requests. Jaquett petitioned on behalf of Robert Kirkwood's heirs as well as himself. He provided a summary of his war service:

> *To his Excellency the Governor and the Honble Council for the Commonwealth of Virginia, Wilmington Del. Jany 18 1831*
>
> *In consequence of a letter from you addressed Col. Mitchell a Senator from Maryland, in the subject of the claim of the late Kirkwood of the Revolutionary army in the State of Virginia, having been place in my hands by Col. Whitely, I beg leave as an old Soldier having equal claims to trespass on your time by detailing certain occurrences, in the month of June last Wm Lambert Jr Esq'r. of Richmond Virginia, atty at law, called on Lieut. CP Bennett [Caleb P. Bennet] and myself, on the subject of our claims on Virginia, observing that under the Laws of that State we were entitled he believed, to Lands, acording to grade in the Virginia Line of the Revolutionary Army, that we would be obliged to attend at Richmond and petition the Legislature to secure the patent &c which could be attended with considerable expence and trouble, that if we would furnish him with the necessary proofs of service in the Virginia Line, and give him a power of attorney to act for us, he would pay all expences and receive one half of the land recorded as his compensation to this proposition, being old and poor and illy able to sustain an undertaking apparently so expensive and doubtful of a recovery, we assented and furnished all the necessary proofs and Documents, duely attested by a Notary under his hand and seal of office, with the Letters of attorney required since which time, we have not a line from Mr Lambert on the subject of our claims, it appears by your letter above refered to that the dispersal of the lands allotted or so to be to*

the officers of the Virginia Line is left solely at the direction and Discretion of the Executive of the State. permit me sir to request the favour of you to inform me by a line through my young friend the Representative from this State the Hon Kinsey Johns Jun'r. if any petition has been presented in the names of Jaquett and Caleb P. Bennett to your Excellency or the Legislature by Mr Lambert and if there is any probability of our obtaining the Lands by this or any other mode of proceedings. I served in the Delaware Regiment from the beginning to the end of the Revolutionary war with Capt Robert Kirkwood, each of our commissions were dated January 4 1776, and I believe neither of us were ever absent from our Reg't. without leave.

I march'd with the Delaware Reg't consisting of eight companies, in April 1780, and attached to the Maryland line under General [Horatio] *Gates. on the 16 August the* [southern] *army was defeated by Cornwallis near Camden, South Carolina and the survivors left in a truely deploreable condition without clothes or provisions. Soon after General Green* [Nathanael Greene, December 3, 1780] *took command of the remains of the army and the Delaware Regiment, by the defeat from eight companies were reduced to two companies of each 96 men, under command of Capt R. Kirkwood, and myself. the senior surviving captains, whome with their subaltern officers were by orders of General Greene, attachd to Col. William Washingtons Regiment of Cavalry as Light troops, and served with them until the close of the war in 1783. I was engaged at the Battle of Guilford Court House* [March 15, 1781], *at Camden* [Battle of Hobkirk Hill near Camden, South Carolina, April 25, 1781], *Eutaw Springs* [September 8, 1781], *the Cowpens* [January 17, 1781], *and assisted at the seige and capture of most of the British Forts and outposts in Carolina and Georgia, to wit Fort 96* [Ninety Six, South Carolina, May 22–June 19, 1781], *Moot* [Siege of Fort Motte, South Carolina, May 8–12, 1781], *and Augusta* [either Fort Grierson, May 23, 1781, or Siege of Fort Cornwallis, May 24–June 1, 1781]. *Thus Sir, I have given you an outline of my services, a time truely which tried mens souls and bodies too. a time of great suffering privation and distress*

I regret to trespass on your time but must plead as an excuse the claims of an old Broken down Soldier of the Revolutionary war. I have the Honor to be with high consideration, your Excellency's very obed't Humble Ser't

Jaquett does not appear on the pension lists for Delaware for the years 1813, 1818, 1820 or 1840. Peter Jaquett assumed a role as a pillar of his community. He was a leader among his veteran comrades and a civic and moral example. He was among the early converts to Methodism in the region. He was a member of Masonic Washington Lodge no. 1, Grand Lodge of Delaware, AF&AM. He was an active member of the Society of the Cincinnati, serving as vice-president from 1795 to 1802.

War of 1812

Once again the old Patriot answered the call to arms in 1812 to defend the borough of Wilmington.[125] During the War of 1812, Jaquett joined the other surviving members of the Old Continental Line, including Dr. James Tilton and Allen McLane, in issuing a statement, which proclaimed:

> *We, whose names are here unto subscribed, citizens of the borough of Wilmington and its vicinity, above the age of forty-five years and by law exempted from requisition to perform military duty, anxious for the welfare of our beloved country, and apprehensive that the crisis may arrive, when the young and active may be called into distant service, do hereby agree to form ourselves into a military corps, to be devoted solely to the defense of the Borough aforesaid, against invasion and in obedience to the constituted authorities, to endeavor to preserve order, promote harmony, and maintain the authority and efficacy of the laws.*[126]

On September 11, 1824, Jaquett was part of the distinguished party that greeted General Lafayette on his tour of America when he visited Wilmington.

In a paper published a century after his death, the author reported, "It was a hard matter for anyone to keep on speaking terms with him. He was a cross, morose, quarrelsome man." He was successfully sued for slander by a neighbor whom he had accused of theft without grounds.[127] Perhaps the war never left him. On one occasion, having lost some wheat, he, without cause, accused a neighbor, a very respectable man, a Mr. Thomas Tatlow, of stealing it, and wherever he went, he was open and loud in his assertion that "Tom Tatlow was a thief."

Tatlow sued him for slander and recovered quite a heavy verdict. The late Judge Booth, who was Jaquett's counsel, in explaining to him his liability for his charge against Tatlow told him that certain language was actionable in itself—that is, if he called Tatlow a thief or charged him with any other felony, Tatlow could recover without showing any special damage, but that there were certain names that he could call him, without rendering himself liable to damages, unless Tatlow could show special damage. This explanation from the judge was the old soldier's chance. He persuaded the judge to put these words on paper, and wherever and whenever he afterward met Tatlow, he would pull out his paper and beginning at the first would go through the roll of names, so long as Tatlow remained in earshot.[128]

Was he a victim of what we today call post-traumatic stress disorder? He certainly experienced physical and economic hardship. Given his rejection by his home state, despite his long and honorable service to the cause of freedom, it might be understandable.

But other accounts depict him as an aging gentleman farmer and self-described "old soldier": "He was one of the ideal patriots of the great struggle for independence and he never wearied of relating the stories of that eventful period, describing many thrilling scenes in which he was a participant. Childless himself, he was a great favorite of children, and loved to relate to them stories of the past."[129]

According to Elizabeth Montgomery's account, "He, so excited, would exhibit his diploma with Washington's signature, and the sword and the gun presented, and the one used in the Revolution, and the other relics; then to promote their pleasure, order the cart and horse harnessed and with youthful guests, hie to the woods for nuts, return in full glee, slip out the tail board, and out the little urchins would pop on the grass much to their amusement. At other times he would fit them with fishing tackle and away to the inlet. Such was his fondness for children, even in old age."[130]

Myths and Legends

There can be no doubt that Peter Jaquett served his country long and honorably. He was wounded on several occasions, although to little effect. At times he was at great risk, and he suffered great personal sacrifices over the course of the war. No one can doubt his patriotism or his courage. He returned to an estate ruined by war and flood.

He lived a long life, and as we have seen, he loved to "hold court" at his estate at Long Hook, entertaining visitors and children. It is not unusual for old soldiers to tell war stories, and it is not unusual for old men to embellish their tales with age. In the author's opinion, some of these embellished tales got taken as gospel and were recorded for posterity by the chroniclers of his time. There is no documentation or proof that he was at Haslet's side at the moment of Colonel Haslet's death. Nor could he have been near Lafayette at Brandywine. There are several accounts and versions of de Kalb's death that call Jaquett's version into question. Some of these confections can be traced to Elizabeth Montgomery's 1851 book, *Reminiscences of Wilmington*, which purports to be a first-person account. It is a charming book full of memories and local lore but an unreliable historical source document in the author's opinion.

LEGACY

Jaquett was one of the last surviving Delaware veterans of the Revolution when he died heartbroken at age eighty on September 13, 1834, only months after his wife, Eliza, had passed. He left no children. He was borne from his home at Long Hook to his resting place, over two miles, by sixty young men of the Washington Grays under Lieutenant Richie, as a tribute of their respect for his Revolutionary services. His funeral was attended by the governor, the mayor and city council and a vast concourse of citizens as bells tolled and muskets were fired. Both Peter and Eliza were buried at Old Swede's Church, Wilmington, Delaware.

A historical marker at Old Swede's Church Cemetery, 606 North Church Street, Wilmington, placed by the Delaware State Society of the Cincinnati, reads:

> *Sacred to the Memory of*
> *Major Peter Jaquett,*
>
> *a distinguished officer of the Revolution Army, who died at his residence, Long Hook Farm, near this city, September 13th, A.D. 1834, in the 80th year of his age, having been born on the 6th of April, 1755. On the fourth of January, 1776, he joined the Delaware Regiment and until April, 1780, he was in every general engagement under Washington which took place in Delaware, Pennsylvania, New Jersey, New York, and the Eastern States. He was then ordered to join the Southern Army under General Gates and with the brave de Kalb he was in the Battle of Camden, of the 16th*

Holy Trinity Church, "Old Swede's," Seventh and Church Streets, Wilmington, New Castle County, Delaware. *Library of Congress.*

of August, in which the Delaware Regiment, consisting of eight companies, was reduced to two only of ninety-six men each, the command of which devolved upon his brave comrade Kirkwood and himself, as the oldest officers left of this gallant band. He was also in the Battle of Guilford Court House, the Second Battle of Camden and in the Battle of Eutaw Springs. He assisted in the siege of '96 and capture of the village of that name, and was also in every action and skirmish under General Green, in whose army he remained until the capture of Lord Cornwallis at Yorktown. He returned to his native state in 1782 and in 1794 married Eliza P. Price, daughter of Elisha Price of Chester PA and as a farmer he lived upon his paternal estate until his death, the brave and honored soldier, the kind and obliging neighbor and friend.

Beneath this stone also repose the remains of
ELIZA P. JAQUETT,
wife of Major Peter Jaquett,

who was born November 25th 1769 and died May 5th 1834. She was an affectionate and devoted wife, a kind and humane mistress and a warm and untiring friend. In early life she became a regular member of the Episcopal Church to which and its ordinances she always remained devotedly attached, trusting to her Saviour alone for pardon and forgiveness and in His gracious promises for the hope of a blessed immortality.

LAST WILL AND TESTAMENT

The will of Major Peter Jaquett was dated June 18, 1834. He provides for a slab to be placed over the graves of his wife and himself and upon which was to be engraved, in addition to the usual dates, his Revolutionary services; he provides a sum for repairs of the old "Trinity Church House" in Wilmington and the stone wall around the churchyard; he bequeaths to his nephew Peter, son of his deceased brother Nicholas Jaquett, his Bible, containing births, marriages and deaths of the family; also his Revolutionary Diploma (of membership in the Cincinnati), signed by Generals Washington and Knox, and his two Revolutionary swords and musket ; he makes bequests to Maria Jaquett, wife of Lawrence Greatrake, and her sister Sarah Jaquett, adopted daughters of his late wife ; Mary Ann Greatrake, wife of Captain Roberts, and her sister Maria Greatrake, wife of Mr. Southerland, and Sarah Greatrake and Lydia Greatrake daughters of Eliza Greatrake; his nephew Peter Jaquett, son of his deceased brother Nicholas Jaquett; to children of deceased sister Susan Alrich; to children of his deceased sister Dorcas Barr; to children of deceased sister Elizabeth Ruth; and to children of deceased brother Samuel. He appoints his nephews Peter S. Alrich and Peter Jaquett, Executors

—Witnesses: James W. Thompson, William Gailey,
*   John M. Smith and James Sorden. Probated Sept. 16, 1834.*[131]

AFTERWORD

*A*nd so ends our story of these two intrepid Patriots. This dual sketch has catalogued their many accomplishments on behalf of their country and their state. These deeds went largely unrecognized and unrewarded in their own lifetimes. The shabby treatment they received in their native state is especially noteworthy and set the lowest standard possible for veterans. Thankfully, treatment of veterans has been much improved in due course over the centuries. Both of these brothers in arms passed in notable ways. Robert Kirkwood died very young, in his thirty-third battle, fighting in Ohio, where he was better remembered than in his home state. As the dean of Delaware soldiers from the Revolution, who enjoyed great longevity, Peter Jaquett was venerated in his community and was accorded honors at his death.

In my research for this book, I came across repeated references to the privation of the common soldier. One is tempted to take note and then move on to reveal the actions of the day or the grand strategy in play. But I ask the reader to take pause and reflect on what it means to march dozens of miles in a day without pay; without proper clothes and sometimes without shoes; without a proper meal; with intestinal distress from eating green peaches; with a fever, thanks to the ague or to smallpox; and with only promises of rewards after the war that prove difficult to redeem. One wonders: what could have motivated these incredible sacrifices?

We owe an unrepayable debt to these men and men like them. The oath these men took was an oath of resolve to remedy injustices and renounce fealty to a king in the cause of independence and freedom. They helped to create the future that we now enjoy. This future realizes a vision of liberty, freedom, equality and tolerance embodied in our Constitution. Today's military oath places that Constitution at the center, which embodies all that we collectively agree on as a people:

> *I, _____, do solemnly swear (or affirm) that I will support and defend the Constitution of the United States against all enemies, foreign and domestic; that I will bear true faith and allegiance to the same; and that I will obey the orders of the President of the United States and the orders of the officers appointed over me, according to regulations and the Uniform Code of Military Justice. So help me God.*

This oath is the code by which our modern military abides. It continues to preserve our freedoms in an unbroken line all the way back to Kirkwood, Jaquett and all those who served alongside them. The nation they helped to create is their lasting legacy to us.

Appendix I

JAQUETT FAMILY
IN COLONIAL WARS[132]

JACQUET, PETER, Ensign. Served in Captain Danford's Company, New Castle County, 1747–48, in King George's War against Canada (Ref. DA-7). "Peter Jacquett Jr." was an ensign in Captain Henry Darby's Company, Delaware Regiment of Continental troops, commissioned on January 17, 1776, and was on duty (in barracks) at Dover on April 12, 1776 (Ref. DA-45). See "Peter Jaquet" q.v.

JAQUET, PAUL, Soldier. Land patentee and planter who paid his quit-rent to the governor in 1669 and whose name appeared on a nomination list of officers in New Castle circa 1675 (list not dated) (Ref. DP-170). "Jean Paul Jacques" received a land patent on March 26, 1669 (Ref. DY-158) (also spelled "Paulus Jaques").

JAQUET, JOHN, Private. Served in Captain Richard McWilliams Company, New Castle County. Enlisted on December 28, 1757, during the French and Indian Wars (Ref. DA-14).

JAQUET, JOSEPH, Private. Served in Captain Richard McWilliams Company, New Castle County. Enlisted on December 28, 1757, during the French and Indian Wars (Ref. DA-14).

JAQUET, PETER, Private. Served in Captain Richard McWilliams Company, New Castle County. Enlisted on December 28, 1757, during the French and Indian Wars (Ref DA-14). It appears there were two men by this name serving in this company.

JAQUET, PETER, JR., Ensign. Served in the Fourth Company Delaware State Troops in Continental service. Commissioned on January 17, 1776 (Ref. DA-34, DA-36) (also spelled "Jaquett" and "Jacquet").

JAQUET, THOMAS, Private. Served in Richard McWilliams Company, New Castle County. Enlisted on December 28, 1757, during the French and Indian Wars (Ref. DA-15).

LEGEND FOR SOURCES

DA—*Delaware Archives, Military*. Vol. 1. Wilmington, DE: Mercantile Printing Company, 1911.

DP—"Delaware Papers," *New York Historical Manuscripts, Dutch*, Volumes 20–21, 1664–82, Chas Gehring, ed., 1977.

JAQUETT FAMILY MEMBERS WHO SERVED IN THE WAR OF INDEPENDENCE

JAQUETT, ANN. See John Jaquett Jr. q.v.

JAQUETT, ISAAC, Private Third Class. Delaware Militia Company, North Division of the Borough of Wilmington, 1778; Private, Captain Morton Morton's Militia Company, 1779–80 (Ref. B-773, C-1083).

JAQUETT, JESSE. See John Jaquett Jr. q.v.

JAQUETTE, JOHN, JR., Private. Captain Morton Morton's Company, 1778 (Ref. B-807). He subscribed to the Oath of Allegiance and Fidelity in 1778 (Ref. O-1778 DSA). Ann Jaquette, spinster, died testate in New Castle Hundred in 1787, naming her brother John Jaquette (Ref I-113). One Peter Jaquett Sr. died testate in New Castle Hundred in 1794, naming his sons John Paul, Jesse and Nicholas and daughters Ann Trent Jaquett, Mary Cairns and Sabrina Murphy. (Ref. I-133).

JAQUETTE, NICHOLAS. See John Jaquett Jr. q.v.

JAQUETT (JAQUET), PAUL. He subscribed to the Oath of Allegiance and Fidelity in New Castle County in 1778 (Ref. B-999, O-1778, DSA). Also see John Jaquet q.v.

JAQUETT (JACQUETT), PETER. April 6, 1755–September 13, 1834. Son of Peter Jaquett (1718–1772). Ensign, Captain Henry Darby's Company, Haslet's Regiment, Continental Troops. Commissioned on January 17, 1776, and in the barracks at Dover on April 12, 1776. Captain Hall's regiment, commissioned on April 6, 1777. Captain, Colonel Otho Holland Williams regiment, Southern Army of the United States, 1780. He fought in the Battle of Camden on August 16, 1780, and was present for the surrender of Cornwallis at Yorktown in October 1781. He was a major in the recruiting service of the Delaware on February 15, 1782, and was a pensioner in New Castle County in 1828. He married Eliza P. Price, daughter of Elisha Price, of Chester, Pennsylvania, in 1794 (Ref. A-34, A-36, A-45, A-90, A-121, A-128, A-467, A-478, B-733, E-212, E-213, C-1343, C-1348; the latter source recounts a detailed petition and statement outlining his military career). He applied for a pension (S46500) from New Castle County on June 9, 1828, as a resident of Wilmington, and he received a bounty land warrant no. 1160-200-30 in May 1791 (Ref. G-18240). He is buried at Old Swede's Cemetery in New Castle County (Ref. H-8).

JAQUETT (JACQUET), PETER, JR. October 12, 1760–November 4, 1816. Son of Thomas Jaquett and Dorcas Grantham. Ensign in the Delaware Militia, commissioned on August 4, 1780, Second Delaware Regiment, to serve in the army of the United States to November 1, 1780. Captain Peter Jaquett married Katherine Longhead (Ref. B-631, C-1348. C-1349, P-366).

JAQUETT, SABRINA. See John Jaquett Jr. q.v.

JAQUETT (JAQUET), SUZANNAH. She made two shorts for the military and was paid on January 6, 1783 (Ref. S-167, DSA).

LEGEND FOR SOURCES

A—*Delaware Archives, Military*. Vol. 1. Wilmington, DE: Mercantile Printing Company, 1911.

B—*Delaware Archives, Military*. Vol. 2. Wilmington, DE: Mercantile Printing Company, 1911.

C—*Delaware Archives, Military*. Vol. 3. Wilmington, DE: Mercantile Printing Company, 1911.

E—Scharf, Thomas. *History of Delaware, 1609–1888*. Vol. 1. Reprint. Westminster, MD: Family Line Publications, 1990.

G—White, Virgil D. *Genealogical Abstracts of the Revolutionary War Pension Files*. Waynesboro, TN: National Historical Publishing Company, 1990.

I—*A Calendar of Delaware Wills, New Castle County, 1682–1800*. Abstracted and compiled by the Historical Research Committee of the Colonial Dames of Delaware. Reprint. Baltimore, MD: Genealogical Publishing Company, 1969.

O—*Oaths of Allegiance and Fidelity, 1778–1779*. Maintained by the Delaware State Archives and the Historical Society of Delaware.

P—*DAR Patriot Index*. Vol. 1. Washington, D.C.: National Society Daughters of the American Revolution, 1966.

S—"Revolutionary War Files." Unpublished, vol. 6. Manuscripts maintained at the Delaware State Archives, Dover, Delaware.

Appendix II

WERE THERE TWO
PETER JAQUETTS?[133]

The *Delaware Archives, Military*, vol. 3, includes a discussion addressing this question. It cites correspondence related to "Peter Jaquet Junr (lately of age)" in 1780 taking the oath of fidelity before Robert Bryan. As an ensign, Jaquett Junior certifies the oath of appointment as Delaware militia in 1780.

One year later, this same Peter Jaquett Jr. certifies the service of John Rogers as a private soldier in McClement's Company of the militia on April 27, 1781.

In 1791, he certifies the service of Joseph Murphy.

As noted in an extract from the State Auditor's Account Book (Report to Legislature), item no. 13: "Captain Peter Jaquet—Lf 2: 9: 10, if due at all, is due to the Senior of that name."

In 1802, the governor appointed and commissioned Peter Jaquet Jr. the first lieutenant of the first troop of Light Horse in the First Brigade of Delaware.

It would seem that this second Peter Jaquett Jr. is younger and affiliated with the militia, not the Continental army. In an undated affidavit of Peter L. Jaquett (grandson), he wrote to his niece:

> *My grandmother, Mary Black, lived through the revolution and knew my grandfather Jaquett who lived at Christina Ferry across from Wilmington Delaware. I myself knew old people who knew him, and it seemed a thing of general knowledge that he was a captain in the Revolutionary War. My father told me that his father raised and equipped a company of troop of*

*Horse as they were called then. My mother read the family history that was
in the house after she became inmate and always was in agreement with the
current reports of his service as Captain. I saw in my early day notices of
Pension that might be applied for. My father said his father rejected all such
in his time and said if they would pay the cost of equipment he wanted
no pension. I knew an old darkey or two that knew my grandfather—one
of them was his slave, the other knew him well, and said he dressed as a
soldier and rode a grey horse and that he saw him yet in his dreams.*

*The farmer, Peter Jaquette at the ferry was evidently my grandfather.
There was not any other place for a ferry or a road to New Castle. The
road from Market Street comes into our old New Castle Road very close.
About the ferry and bridge I will now tell. The ferry where they crossed
the Christina Creek and was the only crossing at Wilmington to go to New
Castle and the only hard or solid ground for a road at the foot of Market
Street and required a causeway (as I know myself) I think or remember
about a mile long, (across the marsh). My father told me there was quite a
strife to get it away from the first New Castle Road. (Afterwards another
bridge was put over at third street the old ferry or old New Castle Road....
Our ferry house, a two-story brick was taken down, it being in the way of
improvements of the town now known as South Wilmington and our nice
old home is gone...)*

*The home of the other Major Peter Jaquette, formerly Captain, is at the
New Castle end of the causeway from the foot of Market Street. The two
Captain Petr Jaquettes lived adjoining places and there is a little confusion
in consequence of names and localities being similar. Major Peter never
lived at the ferry or any other ferry. There was no other place where hard
ground came to the creek to put a road on but through our home place and
no other road to New Castle from Wilmington, but across the marsh near
where it comes to. The old ferry road (I mean Market Street bridge).*

Philadelphia Pa., December 5, 1918
Mr. Walter G. Tatnall
Archivist of the State of Delaware

Dear Mr. Tatnall,

*The Peter Jaquett who took the Oath of Fidelity in November 1780,
was, I think Peter Jaquett, Jr. who was born at Christina Ferry October*

12, 1760 and died November 4, 1816. He was son of Thomas Jaquett and Dorcas Grantham. April 1, 1817, Archibald Alexander was chosen guardian of Isaac G. Jaquett, orphan child of Peter Jaquett Jr., late of New Castle County deceased. (Orphans Court Liber K P. 278) which reference shows that Peter Jaquett was known as Peter Jaquette Jr., although he was the son of Thomas Jaquett. He is distinguishable from Major Peter Jaquett of the Delaware Regiment who was born April 6, 1755, and died September 13, 1834. He was son of Peter Jaquett of Long Hook, New Castle County who was born 1718, and died October 22, 1772, consequently Major Jaquett was only seventeen years old at his father's death and he was never known as Peter Jaquett Jr. Peter Jaquett Jr. was merely in his twenty-first year when he took the Oath of Fidelity, and it may have been due to a mistake that he was described as lately of age, or there may have been misrepresentations of his age due to his desire to take the Oath…

Peter Jaquett Jr., was an ensign in the Second Delaware Regiment it appears by the Roster of Officers commissioned by Gov. Rodney to serve in the army of the United States until the first day of November, 1780, with the dates of their commission and the date applied to Peter Jaquett was August 4, 1780, and you have shown me other documents in which his signature as Peter Jaquett Jr. Ensu. Appears and in all instances is written in a similar manner showing identity.

The half page of account of Isaac Bryan in account with the estate of Peter Jaquett Jr., deceased, which appears to be brought to March 1816, undoubtedly refers to Peter Jaquett Jr. previously mentioned. Peter Jaquett Jr. was also commissioned May 16, 1802, first lieutenant of troop of light horse in the Brigade of Delaware. In the list of open accounts appears "13 Capt. Peter Jaquett the Lf 12:9:10, if due at all is due to the senior of the name." It is claimed by the descendants of Peter Jaquett Jr. that he was a captain during the Revolutionary period and alleged to have been in a troop of horse. It is possible that Peter Jaquett Jr. was elected a captain of militia during the Revolutionary War and that he was known by such a title although he may not have received a commission from the Governor or, if such commission was issued, the record of it may not have been preserved. There is evidence of Peter Jaquett Jr. who took the Oath of Fidelity having been commissioned as ensign. The records suggest two Captain Jaquettes by the allusion to "the senior of that name" and the fact of the tradition of his descendants that he was a captain justifies the inference that he been a captain of militia during the Revolutionary period. His commission in

1802 as first lieutenant of course does not throw any light upon whether he was a captain during the Revolutionary period, but it accounts for the erroneous impression in his descendants that he was a captain of a troop of horse during the revolutionary period.

I appreciate your desire to obtain information to enable you to establish as a fact that there were two captains Peter Jaquett during the Revolutionary period and regret that I am unable to aid you to obtain conclusive evidence of such fact. I think, however, that the evidence justifies the inference that there were two captains of the name of Peter Jaquett during the Revolutionary period, one in the regular line and one in the militia.

Believe me, Yours, very truly,
EDWIN JAQUETT SELLERS [134]

PETITION OF P. JAQUETT

Your Memorilest would respectfully State that he served in the Delaware Regiment attached to the Maryland line under orders of Gen'l Washington in the States of Delaware, Pennsylvania, New Jersey, New York and the Eastern States, from the 4th. of January 1776 Until April 1780, and had an active part in all the actions fought during that time when, the Del. Regt. then consisting of eight Companies, commanded by Col. David Hall & attached to the Maryland line, was ordered to S. Carolina Under the Command of Gen. H. Geats, and on the 16th of August of that year was defeated near Camden S. Carolina, and the Del. Reg. reduced from 8 to 2 Companies. In September the remains of the army where collected & randevoused at Hilsborough in N. Carolina under orders of Gen. Smallwood, Soon after Gen. Green took the Command, when it was found that the Del. Reg. could not muster more than 200 effective men, these by order of Gen. Green was placed under the command of Capt. Robert Kirkwood & Capt. Peter Jaquett as the two Sener Surviving Captains of the Del. Regt. with their Subaltern Officers forming two Companies of 96 men each—see the returns made and sent to the Executive of this State and now in the possession of Thos. Rodney Esq. dated Aug. 30 1780 and signed by Capt. Kirkwood & Jaquett, the field officers and all the other officers except Capts. McKennon & Queenault, Lieut Bennett & Hyatt were killed, wounded or prisoners—the four last named officers was sent to the Delaware State on the recruiting service— in October a small but badly supplied army was collected & organized and again took the feald under Gen. Green, who again Marched us into S. Carolina where after our Victory at the Cowpens we were again obliged to retreat before Gen. Lord Cornwallis to Gilford Court House in N. Carolina where a sort of drawed action was fought. W however on the next day buryed their dead by platoons in the yard of a Quaker Meeting House and left their wounded with our own in the care of the Surgens & Friends, took our final leave of his lordship one taking the rout to Yorke Town in Virginia, and we the rout towards Charlestown in S. Carolina and fought the second action at Camden, the hard and well fought action at the Eutaw Springs, the fortified Court House & town of Ninety Six, fourt Augusta and several forts or fortifyed places we at length Coped the Enemy up in the City of Charlestown, in the meantime Gen. Washington met Gen. lord Cornwallis at Yorke town in Virginia and captured him, and soon after Gen. Washington sent Gen. Wain with a Brigade of the Pennsylvania line to the assistance of Gen. Green who arrived at Gen. Green' headquarters near Charlestown in February 1782 and with them Captains McKennon & Queenault with all the men they had recruited or collected for the Del. Regiment, who had assisted at the Capture of Cornwallis.

About this time the prolimnory articals of peace were signed and hostilities had seaced except a little scarmishing to prevent the Enemy from getting potatoes & rice which they much wanted as well ourselves.

Gen. Green well knowing the privations, fatigue and hardships that Capt. Kirkwood & myself had passed through during our Southern Campayns polightly offered to Send Us home on Command, with orders to the Comesery & Quartermasters Department to furnish us with provisions & forage at every Depot on the road. Capt. Kirkwood left Headquarters two days before me with a view of taking his rout as much a possible by water, and I began my march on the 20 Day february with 4 officers nine involid Soldiers one woman, two waggons and nine Horses but unfortunately your memmorlist found nether provisions or forage in any of the public stores—it is known that the army had not received one cent of pay during all our Southern Campaigns, that Continental money had depreciated 100 for one—and we had a march of more than 500 mile to perform without our pay, rations, forage or one Dollar of the public money, and we could not obtain one single artical of Provision or forage on the whole route without the hard cash layed down, thus situated I did Pay from my own private resources $168.45 as per account rendered of which I have never received one cent, at that time the United States was indebted to me Upwards of 3000 Dols. Exclusive of the sd. amount for pay, commutation of half pay. Depreciation of pay

&c., which was afterwards Payed by giving a certificate which our wants obliged us to sell at a discount of 66 pr. sent—but as it is known that your memorlist had received no pay for the last two years and his patrimonial Estate at first was but very small & that small sum much reduced in the Revolutionary War, it may be asked where he got $168.45 cents he answers that a Noble Harted Lady, a friend of the revolution, of respectable family and fortune furnished him all that money in English Gunies at a time when he had scarsely a Shirt on his back, or means of getting one, or a shoe on his feet, without asking the scratch of a pen for its return that Lady has long since decended to the tomb, but your memmorlist still holds himself in Honor bound to make retrubution to her heirs—Your Memorlist therefore respectfuly asks your Honorable boddy to give him the above sum with interest from the 20 of February 1782, and altho he is too old to fight, he will Pray.

Capt. McKennan & Queenault Lieut C.P. Bennett & Hyatt with all the men &c. all these have descended to the tomb Except Lieut C.P. Bennett, who can certify to the truth of the above statement—I believe there is not an officer now living who served in the Delaware Regiment through the Campaign of 1776, altho there had been more than 80 officers Commissioned and 3500 men enlisted in that regiment Except Yours

P. Jaquett [135]

NOTES

Introduction

1. In the annals of Jaquett genealogy, the spelling has seen several variations, including Jacquet, Jaquet and Jaquett. This is not uncommon, especially when moving from one language and culture to another, never mind the loose and varied spelling conventions of the day. In colonial times, the spelling seems to have settled on Jaquett for the most part, which has become the de facto standard to succeeding generations. In this biography, I have used the spellings as I have found them from various sources. In some cases, there are variations on the same individual depending on the original source. When quoting from primary sources, I have chosen to use their original archaic spelling and syntax, which can be sometimes confusing, but I don't want to risk changing the meaning by "correcting" their English. A detailed genealogy of the Jaquett family can be found in Edwin Jaquett Sellers, *Genealogy of the Jaquett Family*, rev. ed. (Philadelphia, PA: Press of Allen, Lane and Scott, 1907), https://www.ebooksread.com/authors-eng/edwin-jaquett-sellers/genealogy-of-the-jaquett-family-lle.shtml.
2. Patrick K. O'Donnell, *Washington's Immortals* (New York: Grove Press, 2016), 379.
3. Emerson Wilson, *Forgotten Heroes of Delaware* (Cambridge, MA: Deltos Publishing, 1969), 26.

Chapter 1

4. Appointment of Jean Jacquet as Vice-Director on the Delaware; his instructions and oaths of office 29th of Nov., 1655, Petrus Stuyvesant, on behalf of their Noble High Mightinesses, the Lords States-General of the United Netherlands and the Noble Lords-Directors of the General Privileged West-India Company in the same, Director-General of New-Netherland, Curacao, Bonayro, Aruba, and the dependencies thereof, together with the honorable Members of the High Council to All, who shall see, read or hear read these presents, greeting: Whereas we needed, for the direction and advancement of the affairs of the Honble Company and our own on the Southriver of New-Netherland, a proper and qualified person, to command there in our absence and manage everything,

Therefore, upon the good report and information given to us in regard to the person of Jean Paul Jacquet and trusting therefore to his piety, experience and fitness, we have engaged, commissioned and appointed the same, as we hereby engage, commission and appoint the aforesaid Jean Paul Jacquet to be our Vice-Director and Chief Magistrate on the Southriver of New-Netherland as well as for the forts, territories and other places situate upon said river, to keep good order for the security of Fort Casimir and other places, already established or to be established and to give orders and have them observed in all matters concerning trade, policy, justice and military, also in regard to the soldiers, the ships' crews, free persons, high and subaltern officers of whatever position and rank they might be, who are there already or whom we may deem advisable to send there in future; to assist in his position of Vice-Director in the management and command of the places and to keep everything in good order for the service and welfare of the General Privileged West-India Company, to administer law and justice to citizens as well as soldiers and to do further everything concerning his office and duties agreeable to the instruction now given and in future to be given, which a good and faithful Vice-Director is bound to do by the oath, which he is to take at our hands. This having been done, we order and command therefore hereby all and everybody, either servants of the Honble Company or freemen living on the said river or who may afterwards come there, of what nation or position they may be, nobody excepted and especially also the present provisional Commander there, that in our absence they receive, acknowledge and respect, obey, the aforesaid Johan Paul Jacquet as our Vice-Director and Chief Magistrate and give all help, favor and assistance, as much as each may, whereas we thus have considered it advisable for the service of the said Company and the advancement of this province. Thus done and given at our Council meeting held in Fort Amsterdam in New-Netherland under date as above and confirmed with our seal impressed here in red wax.

Provisional instructions for Jean Paul Jacquet, Vice-Director on the Southriver of New-Netherland and the Commissaries joined to him.

The above-mentioned Jean Paul Jacquet is to have, in our absence, supreme command and authority over all officers, soldiers and freemen on the aforesaid river and the forts thereof, the first place and vote in all council meetings, which meetings shall be called only by order and direction of the Vice-Director; in them he shall present all matters concerning the policy, justice, trade, privileges and royalties, the Company and its Noble Administration and conclude by a majority of votes and in case of a tie of votes he is to have a double vote.

5. Jaquette Genealogy, http://genealogy.jaquette.net/ancient%20Jaquet.html.
6. Library of Congress, "Long Hook Farm," 1051 South Market Street, Wilmington, New Castle County, DE, https://www.loc.gov/item/de0163.
7. James Day Howson Jr., "Courage, Loyalty, Strength, Major Peter Jaquett and the Delaware Blues," unpublished manuscript, 5.
8. Francis Vincent, *A History of the State of Delaware* (Philadelphia, PA, 1870).
9. Howson, "Courage, Loyalty, Strength."
10. Library of Congress, "Long Hook Farm."
11. Edwin Sellers, "An Account of Jean Paul Jaquet," *Pennsylvania Magazine of History and Biography* 13, no. 3 (October 1889): 271–80.
12. Maureen Milford, "JFK Assassination: A Legacy, a Loss Unfaded by Time," *News Journal*, November 21, 2013.
13. Old Wilmington, "Kent Manor Inn," http://www.oldwilmington.net/pages-photos/restaurants-1/kent%20manor.html.
14. Reverend Joseph Brown Turner, ed., *Journal and Order Book of Captain Robert Kirkwood of the Delaware Regiment of the Continental Line* (Wilmington: Historical Society of Delaware, 1910), 3–5.
15. Peter Force, *American Archives* (Washington, D.C.: M. St. Clair and Peter Force, 1839), 4th series, 2:633.
16. Ibid., 5:431.

Chapter 2

17. Rick Atkinson, *The British Are Coming*, vol. 1 (New York: Henry Holt and Company, 2019), 445.

18. Joshua Shepherd, "Forgotten Warrior, the Brave and Meritorious Kirkwood," *Journal of the American Revolution* (February 2018), quoting from Kirkwood's journal.

19. John C. Fitzpatrick, ed., *The Writings of George Washington from the Original Manuscript Sources* (Washington, D.C.: Government Printing Office, 1931), 1:271.

20. Ibid., 1:40.

21. Christopher Ward, *The Delaware Continentals* (Wilmington: Delaware Historical Society, 1941), 9.

22. Ibid., 16.

23. David McCullough, *1776* (New York: Simon and Schuster, 2005), 149.

24. "A Little Before Day," in *Personal Recollections of Captain Enoch Anderson; An Officer of the Delaware Regiments in the Revolutionary War* 16 (Wilmington: Historical Society of Delaware, 1896), 21.

25. O'Donnell, *Washington's Immortals*, 90.

26. National Park Service, "The Maryland 400," https://www.nps.gov/articles/000/the-maryland-400.htm.

27. Frank Moore, *Diary of the Revolution* (New York: Scribner's Publishing, 1860), 298.

28. Henry P. Johnston, *The Campaign of 1776 Around New York and Brooklyn*, part 1 (Brooklyn, NY: Long Island Historical Society, 1878), 168.

29. Ward, *Delaware Continentals*, 42.

30. Sir George Otto Trevelyan, *The American Revolution*, vol. 2 (New York: Longmans, Greene Company, 1902), 314.

31. Ward, *Delaware Continentals*, 104.

32. Atkinson, *British Are Coming*, 1:545.

33. Jaquett was reputedly at Colonel Haslet's side when Haslet was killed during the Battle of Princeton, according to legend, but this is unlikely. He was with Kirkwood in Delaware on recruiting duty. Elizabeth Montgomery, *Reminiscences of Wilmington, in Familiar Village Tales, Ancient and New* (Philadelphia, PA, 1851), 91.

34. Ibid.

35. *Delaware Archives, Military*, vol. 3 (Wilmington, DE: Mercantile Printing Company, 1911), 1,358.

Chapter 3

36. George Ryden and Leon deValinger, *George Washington and Delaware* (Dover: Public Archives Commission of Delaware, 1938), 27–31.
37. Wilson, *Forgotten Heroes of Delaware*, 42–43.
38. David Price, *John Haslet's World* (New York: Knox Press, 2020), 197.
39. *Delaware Archives, Military*, 3:1,397–99.

Chapter 4

40. John A. Munroe, *History of Delaware*, 3rd ed. (Newark: University of Delaware Press, 1993), 73–75.
41. John Nields, "Washington's Army in Delaware in the Summer of 1777," Address at Cooch's Bridge, September 9, 1927, 2.
42. *The Writings of George Washington*, from the Original Manuscript Sources (Washington D.C.: Government Printing Office, 1993), http://libertyparkusafd.org/Washington/electronic%20books/Volume%209.htm.
43. Ibid.
44. Nields, "Washington's Army in Delaware," 9.
45. Edward Webb Cooch Sr., *The Battle of Cooch's Bridge* (Wilmington, DE, 1940).
46. Christopher Ward, *Delaware Tercentenary Almanack* (Wilmington: Delaware Tercentenary Commission, 1938), 44.
47. Montgomery, *Reminiscences of Wilmington*, 91.
48. Ward, *Delaware Continentals*, 539.
49. Peter Jaquette, "Pension Application of Peter Jaquette S46500DE," *Southern Campaign, American Revolutionary Pension Statements & Rosters*, trans. and annotated by C. Leon Harris, rev. June 24, 2013, https://revwarapps.org/s46500.pdf.

Chapter 5

50. Mark M. Boatner, *Encyclopedia of the American Revolution* (New York: David McKay Company), 213.
51. Robert Kirkwood's *Journal and Order Book* records, "May 8th, Set sail from the Head of Elk, in Cmpy with 50 sail of vessels, being the Second

Brigade in the Maryland Line, Destin'd for Petersburgh, Virginia at which port the vessel I was in arrived the 23 Inst."

52. Lieutenant Colonel H.L. Landers, FA, *The Battle of Camden* (Washington, D.C.: U.S. Government Printing Office, 1929), 2–4.

53. In 1820, Anderson applied for a pension based on his military service. He stated that he had enlisted as a private in the Delaware Regiment in January 1776, was later commissioned a second lieutenant, became a first lieutenant on May 1, 1781, and served until 1783, having been in twenty-nine battles and skirmishes. Another source shows that he became sergeant major and regimental quartermaster for the Delawares, was commissioned ensign in September 1778 and became a second lieutenant a year later. He was promoted to first lieutenant on May 1, 1780, the rank he held to the end of the war.

54. Ward, *Delaware Continentals*, 334.

55. Otho Holland Williams, "A Narrative of the Campaign of 1780," in William Johnson, *Sketches of the Life and Correspondence of Nathanael Greene: Major General of the Armies of the United States*, vol. 1 (Charleston, SC: A.E. Miller, 1822), 486–87.

56. William Seymour, *A Journal of the Southern Expedition, 1780–1783* (Wilmington: Historical Society of Delaware, 1896), 4.

57. Peter McCandless, *Revolutionary Fever: Disease and War in the Lower South, 1776–1783* (Bethesda, MD: National Library of Medicine, 2007); Cornwallis to Clinton, August 23, 1780, Carleton Papers, https://www.ncbi.nlm.nih.gov/pmc/articles/PMC1863584.

58. Seymour, *Journal of the Southern Expedition*, 5.

59. "The Sacrifice of Delaware's Continental Regiment at the Battle of Camden, South Carolina, 16 August, 1780," in *Delaware Society of the Sons of the American Revolution*, https://dessar.org/cpage.php?pt=45.

60. Joseph Lee Boyle, "The Journal of Thomas Anderson, Delaware Regiment, Part I," *The Journal of the American Revolution*, All Things Liberty, July 25, 2023, https://allthingsliberty.com/2023/07/the-journal-of-thomas-anderson-delaware-regiment-part-1-may-1780-march-1781.

61. Landers, *Battle of Camden*, 54.

62. Ward, *Delaware Tercentenary Almanack*, 38.

63. *Delaware Archives, Military*, 1:622–23.

64. Williams, "Narrative of the Campaign of 1780," 376.

65. Delaware's high casualty rates in the Southern Campaign led Congress to encourage the state to establish another volunteer regiment. However, it was never able to recruit enough men to deploy with the Continental

army. Although engaged in a war, there was no immediate threat to motivate the state's citizens to enlist.

66. Seymour, *Journal of the Southern Expedition*.

67. Wilson, *Forgotten Heroes of Delaware*, 42–43.

68. Sellers, *Genealogy of the Jaquett Family*.

69. Ward, *Delaware Continentals*, Appendix 22, 348–49.

70. Wikipedia, "Johann de Kalb," https://en.wikipedia.org/wiki/Johann_de_Kalb.

71. Ward, *Delaware Continentals*, 350. Christopher Ward makes the case that although the Battle of Camden was a defeat, the Delaware Regiment was by no means annihilated or extinguished. The reduction from eight to two companies is misleading. The remaining forces went on to some significant victories. He notes that in April 1780 it numbered about 350 of all ranks. As a result of many long marches and difficult conditions, there would have been a certain amount of "natural wastage" depleting their ranks. By August, they numbered 275. He calculates the net loss from Camden at about 70 men, with some recovered by Colonel Marion.

72. P. Benson de Lany, "Biographical Sketch of Robt. Kirkwood," *Graham's Magazine* 28 (n.d.): 104.

73. Raymond Wilson, "Delaware Militia," unpublished manuscript, 1940, Delaware Military Heritage and Education Foundation Archives, 6.

74. Jones, "A General History of the Delaware Army National Guard," 25, copy acquired by author.

75. Kirkwood, *Journal of the Marches*, 25.

76. Seymour, *Journal of the Southern Expedition*, 11.

77. Ibid., 13–14.

78. Ibid.

79. Joseph Lee Boyle *The Journal of the American Revolution*, "The Journal of Thomas Anderson, Delaware Regiment Part I," July 25, 2023.

80. Ward, *Delaware Tercentenary Almanack*.

81. William Johnson, *Life of Nathanael Greene* (Charleston, 1822), 443.

82. Seymour, *Journal of the Southern Expedition*, 18–19.

83. Ward, *Delaware Continentals*, 536.

84. Robert Kirkwood, *Journal of the Marches of the Delaware Regiment of the Continental Line in the Southern Campaign*, ed. Joseph Brown Turner (Wilmington: Historical Society of Delaware, 1910), 16.

85. Francis Vinton D. Greene, *General Greene* (Boston: D. Appleton and Company, 1893), 231–33.

86. Ward, *Delaware Continentals*, 430–36.

87. Kirkwood, *Journal of the Marches*, 17.

88. Ibid.

89. Ibid., 18.

90. Ward, *Delaware Continentals*, 455.

91. Shepherd, "Forgotten Warrior."

92. Kirkwood, *Journal of the Marches*, 16.

93. George H. Ryden, PhD, "Delaware Troops in the Revolution," address to the Delaware Society of the Sons of the American Revolution, April 13, 1939, 15.

94. Price, *John Haslet's World*, 203.

95. Ward, *Delaware Continentals*, 536.

96. Cornwallis to Clinton, April 10, 1781, PRO 30/11/5/207–8. This letter is also in Henry Clinton, *The American Rebellion*, ed. William B. Willcox (New Haven, CT: Yale University Press, 1954).

97. Kirkwood, *Journal of the Marches*, 26.

98. Ward, *Delaware Continentals*, 477.

99. Ibid., 541–42.

100. Robert H. Kirkwood Jr. to Washington, March 7, 1783, Founders Online, National Archives, founders.archives.gov/documents/Washington/99-01-02-10790.

101. Ward, *Delaware Continentals*, Appendix 22, 541.

102. Kim Rogers Burdick, *Revolutionary Delaware: Independence in the First State* (Charleston, SC: The History Press, 2016), 138–39.

103. Kirkwood to Washington, April 13, 1783, Founders Online, National Archives, founders.archives.gov/documents/Washington/99-01-02-11049.

104. Wilson, *Forgotten Heroes of Delaware*, 42–43.

Chapter 6

105. Shepherd, "Forgotten Warrior."

106. Richard M. Lytle, *The Soldiers of America's First Army, 1791* (Lanham, MD: Scarecrow Press, 2004), 46.

107. Winthrop Sargent, "Winthrop Sargent's Diary while with General Arthur St. Clair's Expedition against the Indians," *Ohio Archaeological and Historical Society Publications* 33 (1924): 242, 249.

108. Samuel Newman, "Captain Newman's Original Journal of St. Clair's Campaign," *Wisconsin Magazine of History* 2, no. 1 (September 1918): 67.

109. P. Benson Delany, "Biographical Sketch of Robt. Kirkwood," *Graham's American Monthly Magazine* 28 (n.d.): 102–10.

110. Ibid.

111. Ibid.

112. Ebenezer Denny, *Military Journal of Major Ebenezer Denny, an Officer in the Revolutionary and Indian Wars* (Philadelphia, PA: J.B. Lippincott & Company, 1859), 167.

113. Ibid., 171–73.

114. Sargent, "Winthrop Sargent's Diary," 271–72.

115. James R. Albach, *Annals of the West* (Pittsburgh, PA: W.S. Haven, 1856), 639.

116. Shepherd, "Forgotten Warrior." Since the aftermath of the battle, human remains from the site (modern Fort Recovery, Ohio) have been buried and reburied on several occasions. Most of the remains seem to have been interred beneath a monumental obelisk in 1912. The base of the monument is inscribed with the names of various officers killed at the locale, including that of "Kirkwood."

117. Ward, *Delaware Continentals*, 540.

118. Pension application of Hezekiah Foard, S47187, transcribed by C. Leon Harris, and pension application of Guilford Dudley, W8681, transcribed by Will Graves, Southern Campaigns Revolutionary War Pension Statements & Rosters, revwarapps.org.

119. Seymour, *Journal of the Southern Expedition*, 290.

120. Dennis M. Conrad, ed., *The Papers of General Nathanael Greene*, vol. 10 (Chapel Hill: University of North Carolina Press, 1998), 292.

121. Scharf, *History of Delaware, 1609–1888*, vol. 1, 255–56n.

122. Read was in favor of trying to reconcile differences with Great Britain. He opposed the Stamp Act and similar measures of Parliament but supported anti-importation measures and dignified protests. He was quite reluctant to pursue the option of outright independence. Nevertheless, from 1764 he led the Delaware Committee of Correspondence and was elected to serve along with the more radical McKean and Rodney in the First and Second Continental Congress from 1774 to 1777. When the Congress voted on American Independence on July 2, 1776, Read surprised many by voting against it. This meant that Rodney had to ride overnight to Philadelphia to break the deadlock in Delaware's delegation for independence. However, when the Declaration of Independence was finally adopted, Read signed it in August 1777, despite his caution.

123. Burdick, *Revolutionary Delaware*, 138–39.
124. Alexander Hamilton, September 16, 1791. Peter Jaquett, who served in the Delaware Regiment throughout the American Revolution and was brevetted a major in 1783, had unsuccessfully sought appointments from Washington on two earlier occasions (April 18, 1789, and January 16, 1791), Founders Online, National Archives.
125. *Pennsylvania Magazine* 9 (n.d.): 459, in possession of the Pennsylvania Historical Society.
126. Scharf, *History of Delaware*, 280.
127. William G. Whitely, *The Revolutionary Soldiers of Delaware* (Wilmington, DE: James and Webb Printers, 1875).
128. Sellers, *Genealogy of the Jaquett Family*.
129. Ibid.
130. Montgomery, *Reminiscences of Wilmington*, 86.
131. Sellers, *Genealogy of the Jaquett Family*, 130.

Appendix I

132. Henry C. Peden, *Colonial Delaware Soldiers and Sailors* (Westminster, MD: Family Line Publications, 1995), 105.

Appendix II

133. *Delaware Archives, Military*, 3:1,345.
134. Ibid., 1,348–49.

Appendix III

135. Ibid., 1,344.

INDEX

ABOUT THE AUTHOR

Brigadier General Kennard R. Wiggins Jr. (DE ANG, Ret.) is a native of Newark, Delaware. A graduate of the University of Delaware, Wiggins also holds a master's degree from National Defense University in National Resource Strategy. He is a veteran of over thirty-seven years of service to the Delaware Air National Guard and the United States Air Force. Wiggins is on the board of directors for the Delaware Military Heritage and Education Foundation, where he serves as curator for the Delaware Military Museum. He is a history advisor to Wilmington University and to the Pencader Heritage Museum.

ALSO BY THE AUTHOR

The Air National Guard: The Early Years, 1946–1965. Fonthill Media, 2023.

America's Anchor: A Naval History of the Delaware River and Bay. McFarland Publishing, 2019.

Delaware Air National Guard. Arcadia Publishing, 2008.

Delaware Army National Guard. Arcadia Publishing, 2010.

Delaware Aviation (with Jan Churchill). Arcadia Publishing, 2014.

Delaware in World War I. The History Press, 2015.

Dover Air Force Base. Arcadia Publishing, 2011.

Histories of Newark Delaware, 1758–2008 (contributing author). Wallflower Press, 2007.